MORE CHILDREN'S WORSHIP IN THE CHURCH SCHOOL

More
Children's Worship
IN THE
CHURCH SCHOOL

By Jeanette Perkins Brown

HARPER & BROTHERS PUBLISHERS NEW YORK

MORE CHILDREN'S WORSHIP IN THE CHURCH SCHOOL

Copyright, 1953, by Harper & Brothers
Printed in the United States of America

FIRST EDITION

E-C

Special acknowledgment is made to the following authors and publishers who have granted permission for the reprinting of copyrighted material:

THE BEACON PRESS for "The Boy Jesus" by Earl Bigelow Brown, from *Life Goes On and On* by Grace E. Mayer-Oakes.

BURNS, OATES & WASHBOURNE, LTD. for 'The Snowflake" (shortened) by Francis Thompson.

CONNECTICUT COUNCIL OF CHURCHES, INC. for "Thank you, God, for Wondering," anonymous.

CROWN PUBLISHERS, INC. for "Stained Glass Windows" from *Complete Cheerful Cherub* by Rebecca McCann, copyright, 1932, by Covici, Friede.

E. P. DUTTON & CO., INC. for "Sea, Spray, Clouds, Rain" from *Another Here and Now Story Book* by Lucy Sprague Mitchell, copyright, 1937, by E. P. Dutton & Co., Inc.

DR. JAMES ENDICOTT for the story "Lord Show Me One Good Thing That I Can Do."

THE FARM JOURNAL, INC. for "Seeds" from *The Farmer's Wife*, anonymous.

THE FRIENDSHIP PRESS for "We Thank Thee, God" by Frances Hill, and "Easter Surprises" by Edith Lovell Thomas, from *The Whole World Singing* by Edith Lovell Thomas, copyright, 1947, by The Friendship Press.

HARPER & BROTHERS for "This is a Special Place," and "O God Whose Laws Will Never Change" from *Children's Worship in the Church School* by Jeanette E. Perkins, copyright, 1939, by Harper & Brothers, and *Caterpillar, Caterpillar* by Jeanette Perkins Brown, copyright, 1938, by Harper & Brothers.

MISS ADELAIDE HARTPENCE for part of a letter written her in 1952 about the worship of children.

DR. C. IVAR HELLSTROM for the prayer beginning "O God, Giver of life."

HENRY HOLT & COMPANY, INC. for "The Last Word of a Blue Bird" from *Mountain Interval* by Robert Frost, copyright, 1916, 1921, by Henry Holt & Co., Inc., 1944, by Robert Frost.

J. B. LIPPINCOTT CO. for "The Little Bird Upon the Tree," "A Thousand Thoughts," "Great White World," "The Fir Tree," "Pretty Fir Tree" from *For Days and Days* by Annette Wynne, copyright, 1919, by J. B. Lippincott Co.; "Something Has To Come," "Farther Than All the World," "Of All the Wonderful Things I Know," "Oh, It's Nice to Sit and Think of Things," "The Bird Helps the Tree" from *All Through the Year* by Annette Wynne, copyright, 1932, by Annette Wynne.

THE MACMILLAN COMPANY for "Something Told the Wild Geese" from *Branches Green* by Rachel Field, copyright, 1934 by The Macmillan Company.

THE METHODIST CHURCH EDITORIAL DIVISION—BOARD OF EDUCATION for the following from *Boys and Girls*, copyright by Whitmore and Smith: "Seed Song" by Marion Doyle (1940) ; "Christmas Carols" (1939), "The Christmas Story" (1940), "Words with Birds" (1939), and "The Rain" (1935) by Nancy Byrd Turner; "How" by Ann Codrington (1936) ; "The Bethlehem Children" (1937), "O Evergreen upon the Hill" (1934), and "Thoughts and Words" (1939) by Edith Kent Battle. For the following from *Picture Story Paper*, copyright by The Methodist Book Concern : "In October" and "Spring Has Come Back" by Nancy Byrd Turner (1930) ; "Spring Song" by Jean Leathers Phillips (1933) ; "My Song of Helpers" by Ellenore Prince (1936) ; "Today Is Spring" by Edith Lombard Squires (1931). For the following from *Child Guidance in Christian Living*, copyright by Whitmore and Stone: "The Stars" and "The Seasons" by Nancy Byrd Turner (1942) ; copyright by Stone and Pierce: "Planting Time" by Clarence E. Flynn (1947) ; "Autumn Leaves" by Marion Doyle (1946), and "Christmas Once More" by James S. Tippett (1946). From *Pictures and Stories*: "Snow Stars" by Frances Frost, copyright, 1943, by Whitmore and Stone. From *Trails for Juniors*: "Order" by Maud E. Uschold, copyright, 1943, by Stone and Pierce.

4

Library of Congress catalog card number: 53-5435

Library of Congress Catalog card number 52-5432

*This book is lovingly dedicated
to the memory of*
JEAN S. HARDY
*who for thirteen years brought form
and beauty to our Primary Services of
Worship, and whose unusual gifts
with music and with children caused
the period of Music and Rhythms to
be one of joyous release and creativity*

Contents

9

10

11

Trusting Your Dream

Gray winter lies on field and slope,
   And now and then you seem to see
No more of promise for your hope
   Than given for hill or tree;

Yet, on the bleakest day, you know
   Beyond all doubt this shining thing—
That far down is beginning, slow,
   The miracle of spring;

That in the core of every tree,
   And deeper still, at hidden root,
A stir, a pulse begins to be,
   A pledge of flower or fruit.

And just as surely, soon or late,
   A stir begins, an answer starts
(After you learn to work and wait)
   In children's minds and hearts.

Ah, if a winter tree stands true,
   Biding its hour through cold and rain,
Trusting its dream, then so shall you—
   And not in vain!

Nancy Byrd Turner

Part I

Introduction

ADDRESSED TO CLASS TEACHERS AND TO
LEADERS OF CHILDREN'S SERVICES OF WORSHIP

Two earlier books on this subject[1] have dealt with the meaning of worship for children of Primary age, and the atmosphere and conditions which invite it. Experience itself was found to be the basis of all worship, for awe and wonder, joy and thankfulness, love, aspiration and purposefulness all come from within, in relation to what one has seen or known or learned.

The same conditions and principles set forth in the other volumes are assumed in this. Both books were addressed chiefly to department supervisors and leaders who are responsible for that part of the church school program known as the service of worship. Such leaders are concerned that the services which they carefully and prayerfully prepare may really reflect the experience and voice the feelings of the groups they are leading.

That this may be, however, the supervisor must know what is happening in the classes, for the seeds of worship lie in what has gone on in the children's feeling and thinking before they gather in the larger group: what they have discussed, and what the discussions reflect of home and school experiences. The aim of the teacher like that of the supervisor is the development of religious—worshipful— attitudes. The children are learning facts and skills, but the emerging appreciations and relationships are what affect their approach to life.

[1] As Children Worship; Children's Worship in the Church School.

17

This book is addressed, therefore, to teachers as well as to leaders of departments, for it is when teacher and leader work closely together that the opportunities open up for both to strengthen and nourish those worshipful attitudes.

THE IMPORTANCE OF FREQUENT CONFERENCES

Experience over many years in a large Primary department has shown the value of weekly conferences through which it has been possible for the supervisor to know what went on in each class the previous Sunday, to share in the planning of the Sunday following, and to prepare services of worship which would not only take cognizance of each class's interest, but use poetry, art, scripture and prayers made meaningful in classes.

At the beginning of the school year there is always the task of orienting the newcomers, and helping the older children to rethink the reasons for a "quiet time" in the busy morning, and the functions of different parts of the service. The children's own expressions, reported by the teachers, help the supervisor to use materials in her program which she may be sure are on the children's level, since they themselves have created them.

As the year progresses and the various classes enter on their respective interests the teacher-supervisor conferences become even more helpful in the preparation of the service of worship. Often class projects are interrelated, only needing the pointing up of connecting links. Sometimes they are seasonal, and so of common interest. Occasionally the work of one group acts as a challenge to other classes to stretch their imaginations and broaden their horizons.

Frequently a project of one class, dramatized in the service of worship, becomes a departmental enterprise which furnishes a focus for worship for several weeks. Or an idea, a question, a discussion reported by one teacher may be brought before the larger group to become the reverent concern of all. Likewise a poem or a prayer, a litany or a painting from one class or child will stimulate new appreciations in all classes when they gather for worship.

Thus the warp and woof of the services are furnished by the children themselves. It remains for the leader to weave the strands into a design in which new values may be discerned.

A TWO-WAY TRAFFIC—HOW THE TEACHER BENEFITS

But the conference represents a two-way traffic. The teachers, seeing how the worship program is taking shape in the leader's thought, are in a position to anticipate something in the service of special relevance to their particular classes. This enables them to prepare in the children a readiness for interested participation in the service, and to prepare themselves to follow up leads which the service suggests. For sometimes the conference planning introduces new experiences which need further consideration. A visitor from another group may have been invited to talk in the service; slides may have been borrowed from the museum to open the children's eyes to new wonders; or a story which requires much thinking over may have been chosen for telling in the service.

These are often starting points for discussion and activity in classes *in the process of which worship may reach a higher point than in the period designated for worship.* This happens when there is a new awareness of the Source from which all life comes; of the Power which operates so mysteriously and so dependably. It happens as one becomes conscious of the relatedness of things and experiences, and tries to describe that Power (as eight-year-old

19

David tried: "It's what's all around us, making everything one thing"). There is worship in the joyful and loving planning of a surprise for a friend or another group. It is known as one becomes conscious of one's good impulses being strengthened, and as one recognizes and stands in awe before a demonstration of difficult decisions made for love's sake.

So the mood or findings of one period spill over into the other. This is as it should be. Work and worship were never meant to be separated. Frequent supervisory conferences help to make teachers and leaders alike more alert to the possibilities of worship in every experience, and more sensitive to children's readiness for it.

The services outlined in this book are the result of the two-way conferences. It is only through such co-operation, indeed, that worshipful moments in classes and the children's own responses could have been known and used for the enrichment of the department worship.

The book itself is a compilation of experiences with many groups, all of whose teachers it would be impossible to name here. For specific quotations, however, from reports of discussions and creative activities, the author is indebted to the following:

In Chapter I: for "Out of the seed," Mrs. Elsie Koester; for the development of the poem "We Went Out to Find the Wonders" and the prayer-song "Quiet Our Minds," Miss Minna Luckey; for Hawley's impression of the service of worship, Mrs. Romaine Mackey; and for the third-grade analysis of worship, Miss Margaret Lorimer.

In Chapter II: for "Now the Day Is Over," Miss Minna Luckey; for the third-grade responses to "Hilltop in Nazareth," Miss Dorothy Wright; for the ideas for the poem "This Is a Special Place," Miss Elsie Bush.

In Chapter III: for the third-grade's discussions of

light as a symbol, for the lighthouse dramatization and song, and the symbolic Christmas service, Miss Dorothy Wright; for the thanksgiving Litany and musical response, Mrs. Elizabeth Allstrom; for the Christmas Litany, "For Jesus Who Was Born to Mary," Miss Alice Whitcomb.

In Chapter IV: "To Sing and to Make Friends," Mrs. Elizabeth Allstrom.

In Chapter V: for the recollection of Dr. Carver, Mr. Dana Johnson; and for the "Short Story" of Margaret, the Rev. Alden S. Mosshammer.

In Chapter VII: Candle-lighting ceremony, Miss Dorothy Wright.

In Chapter VIII: the Solar System rhythm, the dramatizations of the struggle between good and evil, and of the "Christmas Candles Coming Alive," Miss Dorothy Wright; the report of Dorothy Ann's talk to the first grade, Miss Margaret Lorimer and her assistant Mrs. Elizabeth Clark, and Dorothy Ann herself.

The poetry section of the book represents the combined efforts of teachers and supervisors in their search for materials to cultivate appreciations and quicken awareness in the areas being explored. As they shared their gleanings with one another they now welcome the opportunity to share them with a wider fellowship.

JEANETTE PERKINS BROWN

New York
October, 1952

I

Class Opportunities for Worship

> Truth is within ourselves; it takes no rise
> From outward things, whate'er you may believe. . . .
> There is an inmost center in us all,
> Where truth abides in fulness; and around,
> Wall upon wall, the gross flesh hems it in,
> This perfect, clear perception, which is truth. . . .
>   . . . and to *know*
> Rather consists in opening out a way
> Whence the imprisoned splendor may escape,
> Than in effecting entry for a light
> Supposed to be without.
>   Robert Browning, *Paracelsus*

When a teacher of children, planning for her class, thinks of her task as opening out a way for "imprisoned" truth to "escape," her preparation includes much more than mastering her subject matter. She knows she must create an atmosphere in which discoveries may make a truth apparent; in which a child's insight may emerge and ripen. When this has happened she knows that in that moment of awareness the child is having a religious experience and is close to worship.

It is for this that the teacher in religious education works, knowing that it may not come at a certain time, or in response to one impression. There must be a setting which stirs the mind to activity. There must be time to explore questions and ideas arising out of the subject matter; there must be opportunity to express one's feeling about these in movement, in art materials, or in words.

FROM THE CHILDREN THEMSELVES

The walls of a first-grade room are hung with pictures of migrating birds, both photographs and children's paintings. On the browsing table lies Marjorie Flack's *The Restless Robin*. The children have sung their song describing "The Birds' Year"[1] and dramatized it, ending with the flight to the southland. There are the inevitable queries, "How do the birds know when it is time to go?" "How do they find the way?"

Questioning eyes are turned toward the teacher, but it is not from the teacher an answer comes. It is from Sally Jean, in her solemn pronouncement, *"They were born to know that."* In the silence that follows the others seem to be considering her words. They do not question further. They have come close to Truth and recognized it.

In another first grade, whose room is filled with autumn flowers and seeds, the children are chanting from a chart a verse they have made and to which a more ancient verse has been added which could properly express their feelings:

> Out of the seed comes a plant;
> Out on the plant comes a bud;
> Out of the bud comes a flower;
> Out of the flower comes a seed;
> Out of the seed comes a plant again:
> There isn't any end!
>
> *We can but watch and wonder.*

A second-grade group which has been thinking of the

[1] From *Songs for Little People* by Danielson and Conant.

changes autumn brings calls them "wonders" because of the verses used often in their service of worship:

> Stand still,
> think of the wonders of God[2]

and

> Sing to him, make music to him,
> Go over all the wonders he has done.[3]

They go one day to the park which overlooks the Hudson. As they sit on the benches and make observations, the teacher writes them down. These seem to make a poem, and the children like it when it is read. They add an introduction, that they may share it with other classes, and through it relive their experience.

We went out to find the wonders of the autumn season:

The wind, which swept the trees bare nearest the river;
The little leaf buds on the tips of those branches;
The fallen leaves waiting to be pressed into the earth;
A twig with one leaf—all brown on its edges, and the chlorophyll still there in the center!
So—from green to the brown, and in between the floatings, red and yellow,
Then—the flying away.

The river itself is a wonder:
There are laws about it,
How a boat can float
So all the ships can come;
How the water pushed away
Weighs just the same as the boat;
How God gives us knowing about these laws:
Being able to learn is a wonder.

There is a pattern on the river . . .

Perhaps we will never see so much wonder again!

[2] Job 37:14 (Moffatt).   [3] 1 Chron. 16:9 (Moffatt).

24

The teacher has given her class of city children a first-hand experience of observing nature, and time to reflect on what they see. There is nothing new in it, but together they become so newly aware of a world not made by man that they can say, "Perhaps we will never see so much wonder again!"

So a teacher makes provision for possible worship experiences within the class. They may not happen, but the teacher in planning, hopes they will. She has faith in the "truth within ourselves," and in the children's ability to recognize it, given time and opportunity. She makes provision also for their crystallizing it in whatever way seems most natural. Reporting the experience in the supervisory conference enables the leader to use the form in which it is crystallized as an aid to the worship of the department.

A CALL TO WORSHIP SUGGESTED BY A SECOND GRADE

"Quiet our minds and our spirits," the leader of the worship had prayed when the classes, fresh from their various activities, gathered as a group. "Make us ready for the new thoughts which may come to us here. 'Many, O God, are the wonderful things you have done,'—we would remember them now."

The form of the words for some reason lingered in the minds of one or two second-grade children through the service itself, and even through a rhythmic exercise period which followed. Then came the mid-morning crackers and milk (theirs was a three-hour session). This was preceded by a moment or two when the children were encouraged to close their eyes and wait for beautiful or interesting "pictures" or thoughts. Sometimes these reflected experiences at home or school. Sometimes they were images of something in the story in the service. But this day the ideas came in words.

25

A child with his eyes squeezed together murmured the worship leader's words, "Quiet our minds and our spirits." Another added, "until new thoughts come." A third finished, quoting from the verses used often in the service, and ending as if this were indeed a blessing, "We will go over in our minds the wonders you have done. Thank you, God."

When lunch had started the teacher suggested, "We could make a song from those words," and repeated them. Laurie, on the spot, sang a tune for them which was accepted immediately by the rest of the group, and by many more, for it has been in use more or less ever since in that Primary department. During that "generation," of children it regularly began the service of worship. It is a quieting song, inviting reflection, and setting a mood for worship. (See page 231.)

PREPARATION IN CLASS FOR THE SERVICE OF WORSHIP

The name usually given to the period in the church school session when classes assemble does not, alas, necessarily insure real worship. In fact its name may militate against it. First-grade children promoted to the Primary department may have heard about this mysterious something, which in the kindergarten may not have been named. Their older brothers or sisters may have said, "When you come to first grade you go to the worship." There has been keen disappointment at times that a worship was nowhere in evidence.

This suggests a kind of preparation for the new experience which can be undertaken by the older children. Second or third grades review services which have meant most to them. They analyze the separate parts in order to explain their purpose, and thus become clearer about it all themselves. They try to express their feelings about

26

the worship part of the program. Putting their feelings into words may be difficult, but impressions we wish to give happily do not depend entirely on words.

Hawley, a sensitive third-grade son of a professor, volunteered to explain the worship service to the first grade.

"What would you say?" the teacher asked.

"Well," he answered, gazing dreamily through his glasses into space, "I'd tell them how it's all quiet down there . . . and the music's playing, and . . . oh, I dunno . . . It's quiet down there, and there's flowers on the platform, and sometimes we have candles, and . . . it's quiet, and you can think, and . . . oh, I dunno. Miss —— is sitting up there on the platform, and she makes us feel . . . oh, I dunno . . ."

"Why," said Fred, catching a mood, if not the definition, "he makes me think I'm *in* the worship service!"

There is often a poetic quality in a child's choice of words, e.g., "Praise is praying with a song"; "Praise is praying songs into a tune."

At times the very simplicity of a statement goes to the heart of the matter: "We make prayers because it makes God know we want to do things ourselves." "People come to church because they want to be better than they already are."

These were second-grade responses to the invitation to think about the place and the parts of worship.

A third-grade teacher, who had divided her class into small groups to discuss the meaning and purpose of the service, afterward shared with the supervisor the statements of these groups, transcribed on the blackboard by the teacher. They were in short sentences. (In them one can read the results of the teacher's questions as she pushed back the children's thinking after a general statement, viz., "In prayer we realize what God does." "*What*

27

had you in mind, Bill?" Or, "We have stories about people who are great." *"Do you mean famous, Oliver?"*)

(On the blackboard)

Music

> At first we have praise music,
> We feel quiet and thoughtful and good.
> We feel thankful and joyous and happy,
> We feel like we want to sing.
> All of these feelings tell what praise means.
> (Virginia and Carol)

Prayer

> Prayer is a way we worship God.
> In prayer we realize what God does
>> In making people good,
>> In helping us through the week,
>> In making the world a home for us,
>> In making a better world.
>
> God does so many things for us
> We want to do things for him.
> In prayer we thank him and are happy.
> (Bill and Jean)

Stories and Plays

> We have stories about people who are great.
> They are great in kindness and helpfulness.
> (Virginia and Oliver)

Worship

> Worship gives us a chance to think of God quietly.
> We think about the world he has made;
> About the seasons, and the planets, and the stars,
> And laws that keep it all in order.
> (Joel and Candace)

> We can have stories and sing and pray at home,
> But in worship services we can enjoy them together
> And things are better when we do them together.
> (Jean)

28

The first grade had been looking forward to the visit of this particular third grade who were coming to explain the service of worship to them. Particularly they were looking forward to their first attendance at a service. They accompanied their "elders" to the "worship room" bearing branches of autumn leaves, a chart to which many different seeds were attached, and another with their original verse.

The calls to worship that day were a familiar verse from the Psalms set to music by another group, followed by a "poem" made from some of the ideas the leader had seen on the blackboard. The praise song was familiar. There was a good opportunity to relate another passage from the Bible to the group's own experiences, and to make the first grade feel at home through their participation. The first part of the service, therefore, was as follows:

Quiet Music (leading into the air of a familiar song).

Call to Worship (singing of "Come, oh come, let us worship, sing unto the Lord with Thanksgiving.")

Poem (from third-grade ideas):
> This is a time for quiet thoughts,
> For happy, joyous, thankful thoughts,
> For realizing all God does
> To make this world a home for us
> And make us good.

Thank You Song: "Thank You for the World So Fair."

Leader: This is *an old, old verse from an old, old book called the Bible*, which says "Thank you" in a different way:

Many, O Lord, . . . are the wonderful things which thou hast done.
If I were to count them they are more than can be numbered.
(Psalm 40:5, simplified)

29

Leader's Comments about continually finding something new about the world that "God has made to be a home for us"—full of interesting and curious things; how it keeps us asking questions to find out about them. Mention of red leaves, seeds, plants and how they grow. Invitation to new first grade to tell what they have found.

Seed Chart. Children's explanation of their chart, and the repeating of their "poem," *Out of the seed comes a plant*, etc.

In such ways the teacher-supervisor conferences enable the leader of the service of worship to make use of class interests, activities, and children's original contributions.

II

The Supervisor and the Service of Worship

We can never be sure, of course, what will lead children to worship, any more than a leader of adult public worship knows when his congregation will be led to worship. But there are certain signposts which point directions for the traveler.

One recalls Dr. Fosdick as saying that it was not as he was leading his congregation in the service that he truly worshiped, but while he was preparing for it. That was when he really prayed the prayers which on Sunday morning voiced the thanksgiving, the joys and sorrows, the regrets and hopes of the people in the pews. He had in those preparatory periods actually shared in their experiences and that was what made it possible for these people to participate in the worship. The prayers were *their* prayers. Originally the "Amen" was the affirmation of the congregation, and the dropping of it from most adult services has meant that congregations have lost some of that sense of participation which is a necessary part of group worship.

We who have led services for boys and girls know that unless there is real worship in our preparation our services become more or less "programs." Children are quick to feel and respond to atmosphere, whether it is an impersonal, busy, hectic one, or a serene and reverent one. The leader who understands this, and who has really worshiped in the preparation of the service, has followed one of the directions on the signpost.

31

Participation is another. In place of the "Amen" there are phrases of affirmation which the children can agree upon, and which, at the leader's suggestion, may be used by the group after each sentence, if the children feel that the prayer being made can be their own. There are refrains in litanies. There is the verbal participation when provision is made for the sharing of thoughts.

There is the use of silence. Children have to be trained in the use of it, as most of us must be, but through silent periods a seed-thought sown by something in the service has a chance to flower, or it may find in the soil one which it joins, and a new idea is born, a new insight is gained.

Leaders who are in earnest about leading children in worship will take their directions from these signposts.

SETTING THE KEYNOTE FOR THE SERVICE

The supervisor of a department has a special task at the beginning of the school year. Promotions have brought newcomers to the group. Where churches have closed their schools for the summer, threads must be gathered up, fresh rapport established between herself and the large group, new anticipation and expectancy aroused for the part of the program known as the service of worship. She must set the keynote for services to come.

There may be, at the first meeting, informal exchange of summer experiences which may have led to high moments. There may be reminders of former services, e.g.:

Last year some of you said this about the music we have here:

> There is quiet music,
> And marching music,
> And prayer music.
> The prayer music is quiet, too.

It is the music saying prayers to God
Instead of us saying it ourselves.

Whenever we come to this room on Sunday morning we have these kinds of music. One of you called it a restful time. One of you said it was peaceful. Sometimes we say something like this, "It is a time when we think together about interesting things, and wonderful things; and about people who seem to us interesting or wonderful. Sometimes we have our truest thoughts here, and we tell each other what we have thought."

RESPONSE TO PICTURES

Pictures like Millet's "The Angelus" or Taylor's "When I Consider Thy Heavens" or Elsie Anna Wood's "Hilltop in Nazareth" help to establish the mood for worship. A story, or a report of an incident provocative of discussion helps. Both aids were used with one group early in the year.

The children had entered the service to one of Chopin's etudes. The leader told a story heard during the week of a Quaker mother who stopped her child on his rush out of the house on his way to school. The mother had taken his hand and covered it with hers as she said quietly, "I wonder what this hand will do today." The child had caught her meaning, quieted down, smiled up into her face and asked, "Is this 'Meeting,' Mother?" The leader explained briefly his meaning of "Meeting" and said, "That was all she told me. Why do you think the mother did that?" The responses were many:

It made the little boy wonder.

I think she wanted to tell him to think about his marks and stars, and to be a good boy.

She didn't want him to hurry so, or he'd get all tired out.

33

She didn't want him to run. Perhaps the teacher wouldn't scold him anyway if he was late—he needn't hurry so.

If he was in such a rush he wouldn't do a good job at school.

Maybe he'd forgotten something he ought to remember.

He hadn't stopped to think what he was doing.

Maybe she said that about his hand because he had to do work with it, and he ought to be more careful.

The leader gathered up the children's responses, and compared the mother's wanting to stop the child in the midst of his hurry with their stopping and coming together each Sunday in the middle of the morning. It gave them time to "think what they were doing," to "remember" what might have been "forgotten." She read a familiar verse:

> To this quiet place of worship
> We have come from workday things,
> Pausing for a while, and waiting
> For the thoughts that quiet brings.[1]

Leader: People like a special time to remind them to be quiet, and think, and remember. (Pointed to "The Angelus." Children told what they saw in the picture. Leader spoke of their own church bells, they stopped to listen to the piano rendering of the Parsifal "Quarters." Children said it sounded like "Come to church; come to church." This led into the song from the *Oxford Book of Hymns for Boys and Girls*,[2] "In every town and village the bells do ring" which the leader used as a poem.)

Leader (continuing): In every town and village people come at the sound of bells to do what we call "worship." They have a chance to be quiet, and think about God, what he

[1] From *As Children Worship.*
[2] Also in *Children's Worship in the Church School.*

34

must be like. They think about their friends, and people they love, and who love them. They think of what they have been doing lately. They are not always happy about what they have seen or have been doing. They are sorry about the times when they have not been kind, or helpful or true. They know there are ways to act better, and have time in the quiet to think of those ways. Sometimes they talk to God. It is like talking to a friend. They know that good ideas and strength to act better come from God. They know he will help them. Shall we take time to think now of some of these things?

Quiet

Prayer: May we come closer to you in the quiet, God, our Friend. May we always know you are near and ready to help us. May we be braver, and kinder and truer because of our quiet times with you here, or at home, or wherever we may stop to think of you. Amen.

Sometimes a class teacher takes the picture used in the service back to her smaller group. "The Angelus" bears closer study than can be given from a distance, and was enjoyed in detail by one second grade. The church spire against the evening sky, the full barrow, the hoe at rest, the uncovered head were all noted. When the teacher asked what the man and woman might be saying, Jill responded in short rhythmic sentences:

> Now the day is over:
> Now the work is done:
> It is time for quiet:
> Now we pray to God.

A classmate supplemented, " 'We thank God,' they say; 'we thank God.' "

At another time a picture which had been studied in a third-grade classroom was made the focus in a service of worship. This picture, "Hilltop in Nazareth," shows a boy

35

of Nazareth standing on a hill overlooking the town. His back is toward the viewer, his arms are outstretched toward the horizon.

In the class group the children had assumed that the boy was Jesus. "Why do you suppose the artist had painted him that way, with his back to us?" the teacher asked.

One child thought, "Because nobody knows what Jesus really looked like," and it was "truer" this way. Another said, "Because nobody ever will know *all* about Jesus." Still another said, "He has to be that way because he's probably thanking God for such a beautiful world."

When the picture was used in the service of worship, however, the lad in it was not assumed to be Jesus. He was just another boy like them. When the leader asked what he might be saying, a child's response was like a prayer as he said, " 'O God, we know you do everything!' " His expression was used by the leader in her closing prayer:

O God, we know you do everything! You have made this wonderful world, and have made the life that is in it. You have given us minds to study the rules for your world, and feelings to help us to be kind and think of one another. O God, help us to use our minds well, and to be kind to one another. Amen.

THE SERVICE OF WORSHIP AS A TIME FOR DEEP THOUGHTS

Sometimes the service is interpreted as a time "when we think about happenings, or people, that fill us with admiration, and wonder." One year a leader told of watching for a whole hour the building of a web by a large spider. He had seemed, as he joined one slender thread to another, to fix it with a knot, or perhaps some unseen gluey substance. She could not even guess how he did it. Did the children know any *person* who could make a spider web?

Once the group considered two hinges brought to the service, one man-made, which anyone could manipulate at will; the other a clamshell which the clam could open if necessary, but which was firmly closed as if locked, to a man. Such things point to a Mind that has provided as carefully for the life of the spider and the clam as for the life of a person. They lead to contemplations voiced by the writers who have scattered through books in the Bible wonder verses which enrich our worship.

Mystery is also recognized when stories are told of those who by their courage or their faith, or by their acts of love, reveal a Spirit that seems to the listener almost beyond his comprehension. "How *could* he do that when it was so hard?" "What made her do that, when she didn't have to?"

One September service which referred to both mysteries had begun with music and the reading of a poem made in another year.

> This is a special place to which we come,
> For here we think of special things to say:
> Some make us happy and we want to sing,
> Some make us thoughtful, and we want to pray.[3]

The leader told of a walk and drive in Autumn scenery the day before, when she was filled with "wondering thoughts" and read the poem "Wondering" by Florence M. Taylor:

> I wonder
> How dusty little seeds that look so dry
> Can swell and grow and reach up toward the sky . . .
>
> I wonder
> How feathered wings can lift the birds so high,
> And how birds find their way across the sky. . . .

[3] From *Children's Worship in the Church School.*

I wonder
How dandelions turn from gold to gray,
And milkweed seeds grow wings and fly away;
How green leaves turn to gold and red and brown,
Before the cold wind sends them fluttering down.

Leader: You have probably had thoughts like those, and other
wonderings of your own. It is good to think of them. That is
one reason we take time out of our busy mornings to be
quiet. It is

A time to tell our questionings,
A time to share our wonderings.

I want to tell you about two things that happened to me
this summer that made me wonder, and made me "want to
pray."

(She told of driving down the Redwood Highway, of the
size and age of the trees; how, as the car crawled slowly
along the road between the tall trees, it was like coming
down the aisle of a church—a place to help people to worship, to think of God. She told how she and her friends had
left the car and walked about; how still it was, how they felt
like whispering; how they stretched their arms as the trees
grew—up, toward the sky; how it made her want to grow
taller, too, "nearer the sky"—introducing a familiar song,
"Glad that I live am I.")

Leader (after the song): The second story I wanted to tell you
is a true one I heard about a boy who wanted to be an air
pilot when he grew up. He had been saving his money to go
to a school to learn all about planes. He read and talked
about and and studied the pictures of airplanes wherever he
found them. He stayed for hours in the Transportation
Building at the Fair. Then, this summer he had a bad accident, and lost a leg. He could not be an air pilot after all. His
friends wondered how he would take his loss. How would
he walk? How could he work? His mother wondered if his
disappointment would make him sicker when he knew his

38

leg was gone. When she went in to him she was greeted with, "Mother, I've been thinking. I can't be an air pilot now —but I could be a doctor!"

That story made me "want to pray."

Pause

Leader (continuing): You boys and girls must have had things happen to you too, that you like to think about because they make you feel bigger and better. We can bring them here to share with one another. We can recall them now as the music is being played.

Music; Quiet; Children's Responses

Prayer: O God, from whom our thoughts come, we are often filled with wonder at your world. We are glad you have made us able to admire beauty and greatness and courage. We are glad for thoughts that stretch our minds. As we meet together each week, may we remember that we, too, have in us that which can be fine and great and good. Amen.

III

Children and Symbolism

Everyone familiar with children of Primary age knows how literally they interpret ordinary conversation. They think and speak in direct terms, and words have single meanings. Abstract or figurative language, or parables fraught with meaning for adults, are lost on children. They have not had the years of experience which life has given adults to build up associations with words of different meanings, or with symbolic acts and objects. Associations are necessary for the appreciation of symbols.

Children feel this necessity, for they strain to follow their elders' speech, trying to make their own connections with unfamiliar words. The results are often fantastic. We can still hear the lusty voices in a country Sunday School singing the old Gospel hymn, "Ri-i-ng out the watchword," and feel some of the enthusiasm with which one child joined in the adults' "worship." But the child was singing words that made sense to her, and sounded enough like what she had heard. Her words, "Wring out the washrag," were quite satisfactory.

We recall, too, the six-year-old's interpretation of a sermon on the wise and foolish virgins. "There were these ladies," he explained, "and they ran out of gas."

Are we, then, justified in using symbols or figures of speech in children's services of worship?

The significance of any symbol, even for adults, lies in our understanding of the reality back of it, and our feeling of its appropriateness in standing for that reality. Children do think and speak directly, but they also think and play in the language and world of symbols. One thinks of the six-year-old's anthropomorphic play, and the eight-year-old's delight in secret codes. We must bear in mind, however, that these symbols are the children's own, having meaning because created or adopted (after understanding) by them.

Other symbols, like the swastika during Hitler's regime, or our own flag, for instance, have had the power of calling forth jeers or cheers, according to the associations which have been built up in the children's minds. As symbols, then, they are effective even to small boys and girls; they have been interpreted in terms understandable enough to call forth an emotional response.

Religious art and worship for adults lean heavily on symbolism. Heaven is a symbol. Angels are symbols. The cross is an almost universal symbol whose meaning grows with man's experience. Our worship is richer for words and signs which not only have had traditional significance, but to which each person can add his own associations, perceptions and emotions.

Symbolism is like poetry: it gives form to thought and expression to feeling; it makes seem tangible what must forever remain intangible; it deepens insight and stirs emotions.

We believe it has value in children's worship if intelligently and sparingly used. It introduces children to a means of expression whose value they may increasingly appreciate and employ when a truth, an ideal or an idea waits to be made concrete with word or imagery or action.

41

Perhaps the most common and effective symbol which may be used with children, one around which many associations may gather naturally, is Light.

Most boys and girls have had candles on a birthday cake. Thus the approach to symbolism has already been made. Each candle *stands for* a year of the child's life.

Children may have seen lights on the altar of the church, or in another sanctuary. Have they ever thought about what these stand for? They may have heard of the Jewish Feast of Lights, or been present at some candle-lighting ceremony. They may have seen in the place of worship of one of the other departments a seven-branch candlestick, or a single lighted candle on a stand. Any one of these experiences may be in the background of a child or a group, and start thinking or discussion about the significance of light.

Or an approach may be made through pictures. Artists of religious subjects are fond of using light symbolically. Haloes are often a subject of curiosity, and the questionings of one class may well be brought before a whole department, and lead to discoveries of other ways in which people have used a symbol to represent an idea.

EXPERIENCES AND CREATIVE ACTIVITIES AROUND LIGHT

Through the years in one church, teachers have been interested to see the appeal that "light" has made to Primary children when the use of lights in worship has invited interpretation. The children like to think about light, and talk about it. It is beautiful and mysterious and powerful, and suggests different experiences to different people. It has become so full of associations and meanings that light symbolism has appeared again and again in third-grade poetry and programs, while younger children in their litanies and songs have thanked God for the life and safety and joy and beauty which light creates. There are stories which have become favorites through the years.

First- and second-grade children have experimented with light, watching lima beans which failed to sprout in the dark, while others thrived in the sun. They have made "shadow sticks" to record on the bases the lengthening shadows cast by the sun through the year and they have enjoyed the colors in prisms as the light rays were broken up. These and the children's home experiences (brought into the service) have formed the basis for some of the thinking about light: its laws and its uses, its beauty and its symbolism; and the references to light in the service have in turn stimulated activities in the classes. Third-grade children have patiently dipped—and dipped—their O-cedar mop wicks into bayberry candlewax to make candles for gifts at Christmas; spent time on other Sundays making clay candleholders, and then used candles and holders (before presenting them to parents) in original candle-lighting ceremonies in Christmas services of worship.

Some of the materials used and developed by these groups may be suggestive to other departments interested in light.

A SERVICE INTRODUCING SYMBOLISM:
BUILDING UP ASSOCIATIONS

On a Sunday early in the year a seven-branch candlestick, with candles unlighted, is on a low table at one side of the platform. In the center of the platform, on an easel, is Taylor's picture, "When I Consider Thy Heavens."

Speaking of the many groups of people gathered for worship in many places, the leader shows the drawings and paintings of different kinds of churches. These have been made in one third-grade class, to recall churches attended or seen during their summer vacation. They range all the way from a clapboard meetinghouse to a stone Gothic cathedral, and when the leader asks what the buildings were like inside, the children tell of "pretty colored windows," or "writing on the wall," or "organ pipes with a design on them." Some had "a cross up in front"; most of them had flowers, some, candles. Why do the children suppose people like to have flowers, or plan for colored windows, or have candles, she asks. After one or two answers she suggests a sort of game.

She mentions three words, after each of which the children are asked to raise their hands the moment a picture comes to mind. The words are: *Water, Darkness, Light.*

For *Water* the children mention such things as "Boats," "Swimming," "Glass," "Bridge," "Ripples."

For *Darkness* they see "Black," "Night," "Ghosts," "Sleep."

To *Light* they respond with "Day," "Sun," "Stars," "Flowers," "Blue sky."

To the question, "How does light make you feel?" they answer, "Happy," "Gay," and "Safe."

Leader: Do you think the candles used in the churches you saw this summer might mean some of these things to people worshiping there? We often use pictures or objects, to remind us of something. They "stand for" a special thing in our minds, just as "water" stood for "boat" for one of you, and "swimming" for another.

When we use something to remind us of something else, we call it a sign, or a symbol. Some of you like to use what you call sign language. It isn't the language you speak in, but one in which certain signs stand for certain words or ideas. Each sign is a *symbol* of a word or idea. So the carving

44

and pictures and lights we see in churches are symbols: they are put there to remind people of a happening, or a story, or a person, and to bring back a feeling they may have had about the happening or the story or the person.

We might be thinking this week more about light and why it is used in so many churches. Could it be standing for something?

Introducing a Story: There was a boy once who used to think a great deal about light—particularly the lights in the sky (pointing to picture). He often had the same feelings about them, that people have in church. See if you think his lights in the sky and candlelights in church might bring some of the same thoughts to mind.

Story: of Michael Pupin, the herdsman's boy, who watched the stars at night. When they were in a certain position in the sky it was as if they spoke to him. He felt as if it were a message from God, saying: "Watch carefully, this is the time of night when the cattle like to stray into the neighbor's field of corn." When sunrise came again it was once more as if God were speaking to him, saying, "It will be easier for you to watch, now that the sun's light has come." Michael's mother read Psalms to him from the Bible, and taught them to him. His favorite one was about the sky and the day and the night, because it spoke of the light traveling all over the earth carrying messages without words.[1]

Reading from Psalm 19 (Moffatt or R.S.V.).

Music (introduced by its title): "The Evening Star" from *Tannhäuser.*

Prayer (based on children's previous responses): O God, from whom all light comes, we thank you for sunlight and day-time, flowers and blue sky. Light makes us feel glad and

[1] The story from Michael Pupin's *From Immigrant to Inventor* is retold for children in *Children's Worship in the Church School.*

safe. We thank you for the starlight, and for the thoughts that come to us as we look into the sky. Amen.

THE SECOND SUNDAY

The Taylor picture today is on the easel at one side of the platform, but the seven-branch candlestick (with candles still unlighted) is on the table at the center.

The "Moonlight Sonata" is being played as the children come into the room and sit quietly.

The leader speaks of the way some of the Psalms might have been composed, one or more persons naming the reasons for, or objects of, their gratitude to God, then all the people joining in a refrain of thanksgiving. She reads from Psalm 136 (a.s.v.), which mentions "lights" and invites the children to join in the refrain:

> Oh give thanks unto the Lord: for he is good;
> *For his lovingkindness endureth for ever.* . . .
> To him who alone doeth great wonders;
> *For his lovingkindness endureth for ever:*
> To him that . . . made the heavens;
> *For his lovingkindness endureth for ever:*
> To him that spread forth the earth. . . .
> *For his lovingkindness endureth for ever;*
> To him that made great lights;
> *For his lovingkindness endureth for ever:*
> The sun to rule by day;
> *For his lovingkindness endureth for ever;*
> The moon and stars to rule by night;
> *For his lovingkindness endureth for ever.*

FROM REALISM TO SYMBOLISM

The first-grade children had been talking in their class of all the kinds of lights they could think of from bonfires to flashlights, and spoke of them now when the leader asked if anyone had been thinking more about lights.

She suggested that they all think together of the good that light does, and the responses ran from the obvious and more or less expected, "It makes things pretty," "It helps you see," "It gives you energy," "It makes you strong," "It makes the red blood in your veins," "It makes you safe" (guiding airplanes and ships), "It heals people" (X rays and radium), to the less obvious and wholly unexpected, "It makes you good!" The child elaborated: "There are good feelings and bad feelings inside you. The bad feelings are like the darkness, and the good are like the light that drives away the darkness, and that's like a candle, that tells you what to do."

They were back to candles again, this time with symbolism of their own making. Perhaps light always gave people thoughts of strength and healing and beauty and goodness, the leader suggested, and that was why it was used in churches, where people come to think about God and goodness, and the choices we have to make between good and bad. "We could have candles, too, in our service," she went on, "if it would help our thoughts. Each one of the candles, or the light of all together, might stand for something you would like to be reminded of here."

At this point the leader lighted a taper, with which children, one by one, as they came to the platform, lighted the candles, explaining what it should stand for.

"It makes me think of angels," a boy said. "The glow around the candle flame is like the round light around the head of an angel, or of Mary in pictures." Another time they would talk about haloes, and angels, and the symbols an artist uses to make us know how he feels about a person or an event. Today they would listen to some music by Grieg, which would follow up the idea of good and bad feelings with its contrast of light and dark. The music supervisor always seemed to have the right music on hand.

47

This service closed with a litany making use again of some of the children's responses, and a refrain for which they had previously made a tune:

Litany: O God, from whom all light comes, we thank you for the light of day, the lights of night. We thank you for the brightness of the sun and the beauty it brings.

> [*Refrain:*] 1 Chronicles 16:9.

We thank you for candles, and electric lights, and for bonfires which have somehow caught the lights of the sun.

> [*Refrain*]

We thank you for giving us feelings, and for speaking to us through our feelings, which are like a light to guide us.

> [*Refrain*]

THE THIRD SUNDAY

The seven-branch candlestick was the only decoration on the platform. When the music stopped there was the usual hush as the candles were lighted, one by one, with their symbolic meanings given. The leader said she would make a prayer from the thoughts the children had given: They could join with a familiar refrain.

Prayer: O God, we thank thee for light,
            Because it is pretty,
            Because it drives away the darkness,
            And helps us to see;
            Because it gives energy and health,
            And helps us to travel safely;
            Because it makes us feel happy,
            And think of good things.

> [*Refrain:*] *We thank thee, O God.*

            We thank thee for our church
            Where we can be quiet

And think of beauty and light
And have new thoughts about thee.

[Refrain:] We thank thee, O God.

The story today was of Brother Francis who had sung his "Canticle to the Sun." Incidents from his life were told by third-grade children who were learning about him, and who sang the song in the service, after introducing it and promising to teach it to the other classes.

A STORY FOR THE FOURTH SUNDAY

This was introduced, after listening to music, and lighting the candles, by suggesting that the children try to remember all of the things of which light reminded them. "Perhaps the story will give us another thought about light."

THE LITTLE GIRL WITH A LIGHT

A few years ago a man and a woman stepped off the train in New York and looked around them. They seemed to be very anxious and in a great hurry.

"Come," said the man, "we must lose no time," and lifting the bags, he hurried ahead. A porter stepped up to them.

"May I help you, sir?" he asked. The traveler stopped.

"Yes," he answered, "I am sure you can. Will you tell me the very best way to get to Ellis Island, the place where the ships stop when they come into the harbor? Our little niece has come all the way from Germany alone, and is waiting for us there."

The porter whistled. "All the way from Germany alone!" he said. "I reckon she will be frightened not to find you there. Does she get scared easily?" He had lifted the bags and was leading the man and the woman out through the gate. The woman answered him.

"We don't know, we have never seen her. Her mother has sent her over to us, thinking she will be safer here. We must get to her as quickly as we can."

49

"Well, the quickest way, Ma'am, is the subway," said the porter. "Subway to South Ferry, and then get the ferry boat to Ellis Island. I'll put you on the right train. Kind of sorry for that little girl, all alone; reckon she's about crying her eyes out about now!"

The man and the woman sat down with their bags around them and the train started. The woman was almost crying herself.

"Think of Elspeth being here nearly a week," she said, "and having nobody to take care of her. Oh, I wish the train would hurry!"

It seemed a long time before it stopped at the station where the porter had told them to get off. Before they could board the boat that went to Ellis Island they had to answer some questions and get tickets. When the boat started at last it seemed as if it would never reach those big brick buildings which they could see in the distance, out in the bay. The great Statue of Liberty, too, was in sight, but they hardly looked at it. All they wanted was Elspeth, their little niece, whom they had never seen, but who had come to live with them because of the war. "Dear child," they kept saying, "how lonely and frightened she must be! What a pity we did not get word of her coming before!"

The boat stopped and they went ashore. They walked toward a man at a tall desk.

"We have come to get our little niece," Elspeth's uncle said. "She has already been here a week."

"What is your name?" the man at the desk asked, "and what is the child's name?"

"My name is Henry Firman," said Elspeth's uncle, "and the child's name is Elspeth."

"O-oh," said the man at the desk, "the little girl with the stars in her eyes! Well, she will be glad you have come, but they will miss her in there."

Elspeth's aunt and uncle looked at each other. They wondered what the man meant. They filled out some papers and then were sent to a big room with rows of benches in it. Women were working there. Leading out of the room was a long corridor and in the corridor they could see children seated at tables. A woman who seemed to be in charge came toward the visitors.

"We have come for our niece, Elspeth," explained Elspeth's uncle. "She has been here a week, but we did not know."

"Ah," said the woman, "Elspeth is your niece? We call her the little girl with the light."

"So?" answered Elspeth's uncle. "Why is that?"

"You do not know her, then," said the lady. "Come, you will see."

She led them to the door opening into the corridor. The children were sitting at desks, looking at picture books, or playing in the sand table, or putting pegs in boards. A very small child was crying and an older child with pale yellow curls and a doll in her arms was bending over her, comforting her. Before long the little child was laughing and had started playing a game of slapping hands, like Pease Porridge Hot, with the fair-haired child and her doll.

"That is Elspeth," said the lady. "They all love her. She has been cheering up all the little children here ever since she landed. She must have been lonely herself, but when someone asked her one day, she said, 'No, I have Nana.' Nana is her doll, the only treasure she brought with her from Germany. Yet she lets one lonely child after another play with it. Elspeth!" she called.

The fair-haired child looked around with a smile on her lips and in her eyes that made her uncle and aunt say "Oh!" She looked from one to the other, and then, with the doll in her arms, came running to them. There was truly a light in her eyes, and her face fairly shone as she said, "My aunt and my uncle?"

"Yes," they said, and held out their arms. She ran into them, putting her arms around first her aunt and then her uncle. Then she said,

"This is Nana; will you kiss her too? She is glad you have come." So they kissed Nana.

"Are you ready to come with us?" they asked.

"Yes, I have been waiting," said Elspeth simply. But she looked at the little girl who had been crying. Her face now was all puckered up.

"It's Maria," explained Elspeth. "She is unhappy; she will be lonesome when I go." As if the little girl in the corridor could hear, she began to cry loudly.

"Come, we had better go quickly," Elspeth's uncle said kindly. "Have you anything to take?"

"Only Nana," said Elspeth, "and my bag of clothes." She looked up into his face. "I am glad you have come. Nana and I are glad." They turned to go.

Maria's wail rose louder and louder. Elspeth hesitated. Suddenly her hand slipped from her uncle's big one, and she ran into the corridor toward her little friend. The wails became less loud, and finally stopped altogether. Elspeth skipped out again, her eyes shining, but her hands empty.

"Where is Nana?" asked her uncle.

Elspeth's eyes were very wide and very blue as she looked up and said, "I left her with Maria. Maria has nothing. I have you now, I shall not need her so much," and she smiled again. Her eyes were bright.

"You see why we call her 'The little girl with the light'?" asked the friendly woman, and she gave Elspeth a good-by hug.

"We see," answered the uncle, as the little girl skipped beside him.

"I think," Elspeth's aunt said to the friendly woman, "the light is inside Elspeth."

IN THE CLASSES

In the meantime discussions in classes were clarifying and enriching the children's thinking about symbolism. The first grade had planted some seeds, and talked about their "sleeping" and having "secrets about growing" inside them, and how, as they grew, they could tell a kind of story. The poem, "Do you know? Have you heard?"

(page 200) was used, and the children themselves made up the story the seeds told.

In the second grade, Taylor's picture of the night had stimulated talk about the stars, and the story, "The Constant Star," by Alice Geer Kelsey, told in another service, was supplemented by the appreciation of the star poems of Frances Frost and Nancy Byrd Turner (page 191, 192).

In a third grade a poster for a cancer drive had been brought to class one day and discussed. The poster had a sword and a candle design! What did a sword or a candle have to do with helping to drive out cancer? The children said you couldn't really kill disease with a sword, but the sword showed that you had to fight it. The candle could stand for "the knowledge doctors have to have, to fight it right."

The next week the teacher of this class quoted the words of John Ruskin: "Every truth we know is a candle given us to work by," and they applied the words to the poster. They discussed the kinds of truth which that particular candle would stand for, then the kinds of lights in the world which are used for guides (lights on airports, in lighthouses, etc.). The class had visited a Succoth booth in the neighborhood and talked about the symbolism in the open space left at the top. Did the Hebrews in their leafy booths need the stars for physical light? It was decided that those stars, too, were the symbol of a spiritual inner guidance for which they were looking. The teacher referred to the Quakers again, and their dependence on the "Inner Light." The teacher asked what the children thought this meant.

Oscar said, "It's minds and ideas." "I think it's knowledge," was Tommy's response. Jill called it conscience: "It's conscience; it's really the Jiminy Cricket in Pinocchio." Judy said, "It's God."

53

They played with the idea of outside lights which are guides and the Inner Light and compared their likeness and their difference. They might all be guides, of a kind, the teacher suggested, but asked if some went out while others lasted. Oscar referred to the story of Johnny Appleseed which had been told in a service of worship. "The life in the appleseed, of course, is still going on, and we just don't know what a long, long time it's going to go on. I guess inner lights, like ideas and life, go on much longer than outside lights that we make."

They talked of the many changes that occur with outside lights, of times when they disappear, and the teacher, sure by then that the children understood the symbolism they had been using, suggested their writing a poem to sum up in a brief way all they had been feeling and discussing. Their poems became a part of the Christmas service. This class enjoyed using "light" symbolism throughout the year. It kept cropping up in discussions. It led to a dramatization for the younger children of the story of "The Little Red Lighthouse and the Great Gray Bridge." It suggested interesting movements in their rhythm period. (This period is described in Chapter VIII.) One of these was worked out by the children for an Easter service; it was the theme of their final prayer, which they set to music:

> The light from the lighthouse guides the ships;
> The lights from the bridge the airplanes see;
> Light, Light, *standing for Goodness,*
> Please come inside to guide me.

THE THIRD-GRADE'S SYMBOLIC CHRISTMAS SERVICE

When this class asked to make candles for Christmas and "have a service about lights Christmas Sunday," which they "made up themselves," there were in the classroom four different pictures of Jesus talking with listening groups. As the children were studying the one of Jesus preaching from a boat, the teacher asked what they thought he meant when he said, "Ye are the light of the world."

Many were gathered on the shore, in the picture, men and women of different types, and children as well.

"I think he meant, 'You people who understand these ideas I've been telling you,'" Oscar ventured, while Joy added, after some discussion, "You see, they carry those ideas on, and the ideas are like a light to show people what to do."

The framework for their Christmas service was thus suggested. The children studied the pictures closely, noting the expressions on faces. They imagined the professions and backgrounds of the figures portrayed, and their different reactions to Jesus' words, some of which, like "Love your enemies; do good to them that hate you," were on the blackboard. The December services of worship, planned to give children an appreciation of the man whose birthday they would presently celebrate, contributed to the discussions.

Finally, each child chose one character in the picture to impersonate in their Christmas service. The story of how Phillips Brooks wrote his hymn, "O Little Town of Bethlehem," with its words:

> Yet in thy dark streets shineth
> The Everlasting Light

had suggested having one large candle "that stays lighted all the time." "We'll say that the big candle stands for the ideas of Jesus, and then each one will tell who he is and light our candle from that one."

So the service took shape. It was held in a large room

with a fireplace. A fire burned brightly, a lighted Christmas tree was at one end of the room, and one lighted candle on a silver-covered box pedestal at the other. (The pedestal was a little high, but by this time Oscar was so used to thinking in symbols, he took even the supervisor's mistake as a symbol!) The service follows:

Quiet Music as children entered and seated themselves on the big rug (as near to the Christmas tree as possible!): Victrola record, "Sheep May Safely Graze." (The children softly commented on the fire and candlelight; the room would have been quite dark without them.)

Poem (introduced as having been made by Christine in a third grade):

> Flowers for Christmas!
> Beautiful flowers
> For Christmas eve.
> Lights for flowers!
> And singing from heaven
> To earth.

Songs: "O Come All Ye Faithful" and "Silent Night."

Story (simply told, for first grade): The First Christmas.

More Carols: "Come Softly, Tread Gently" and "O Little Town of Bethlehem."

Leader (introducing children's symbolic poems): We like to think about lights in our service. One of the third grades has been thinking about light in its class. The boys and girls have talked about lights as symbols. They thought of them as guides. It made Tommy think of the light on our church tower, and what it might mean.

Poem (read by Tommy):

> There's a red light at the top of Riverside Church.
> Red lights usually mean "Stop."
> I think Riverside Church is signaling
> For people to stop and think.

Oscar's Poem:
>There's a light on top of the tower of our church;
>It might guide people's thoughts
>To better living,
>And to God.

Joy's Poem:
>>The city lights we see
>>Give many thoughts to me
>>Of people inside different homes;
>>Of people working late at night,
>>Of people whose ideas and thoughts
>>Are inner lights that glow
>>And guide the world.

Leader: The class talked about how some lights go out, but that other lights keep right on. They made another poem.

Group Poem, "Two Stars" (read by Judy):
>A star outside—an inside star,
>Both show the way.
>The outside star can move away,
>Or be hidden by dark clouds,
>Or smoke from guns,
>Or many airplanes dropping bombs.
>The inside star is always there:
>It's knowledge—conscience—love, and God.

Leader: Jesus is sometimes called the Light of the World. This class has been thinking why; and yet there is a story about Jesus in which he called some other people the "light of the world." The boys and girls in this class have been thinking especially about that as they have made their candles this Christmas, and planned this service around it. They asked to have one candle burning all the time. They were thinking about Jesus being the "Everlasting Light"—the "Light of the world"—but their service now is going to show who they think Jesus meant when he called some listeners the "Light of the World."

Tommy (standing by the table with the tall, lighted candle):
Jesus was talking to a group of people. Many kinds of people
were there. He said to them, "Ye are the light of the world."
We think he meant "you people of all kinds who understand
my ideas. You carry with you the light of my ideas."

Judy: I am a *shepherd.* I like to care for all helpless animals
and guard them. I think Jesus meant me. (Lighted her
candle and left room.)

Wendy: I am a *doctor.* I help all people who suffer, rich and
poor, young and old people in my country, and people from
all countries. I think Jesus meant me. (Lighted candle and
left.)

Joy: I am a *worker.* I work in fields, in mines, on boats and in
homes. I work hard and get very tired sometimes, and sometimes people are cruel to me, but I do the best work I can.
I think Jesus meant me. (Lighted candle and left.)

Babette: I am a *child,* the kind of child who wants to learn. I
think Jesus meant me. (Lighted candle and left.)

Ingeborg: I am a *father,* the kind of a father who teaches his
children to be like Jesus. I think Jesus meant me. (Lighted
candle and left.)

Charlotte: I am a *mother,* a mother who is so kind herself that
her children understand what Jesus meant by kindness and
love. I think Jesus meant me. (Lighted candle and left.)

Oscar: I am an *old man.* I have learned during my life how to
be kind. I pass on the ideas of Jesus to younger people who
carry them on and on. I think Jesus meant me. (Lighted
candle and left.)

Sylvia: I am a *young man,* who listens to those ideas of older
men and passes them on. I think Jesus meant me. (Lighted
candle and left.)

58

The tall candle remained lighted, but the small ones were extinguished in the hall outside, and the class came back in their own characters and joined in the singing again of "O Little Town of Bethlehem," and the following litany (borrowed from children from a weekday group in the city, and previously used in the other third grade):

Litany:

For Jesus who was born to Mary on the first Christmas,

[Refrain (sung):] *We thank thee, O God.*

For the beautiful star that lighted the sky,

[Refrain:] *We thank thee, O God.*

For the custom of keeping Christmas, which has lasted through the years,

[Refrain:] *We thank thee, O God.*

For Christmas trees and their lights which have become a beautiful symbol,

[Refrain:] *We thank thee, O God.*

For churches where we can go to remember the real meaning of Christmas,

[Refrain:] *We thank thee, O God.*

Song: Oh, sing to the world that love is born
            At happy Christmas time!

Music (as children left the room): "O Little Town of Bethlehem."

OSCAR FINDS MORE SYMBOLISM

"You know," commented Oscar after the service, "I think Mrs. B. had put the candle standing for the ideas of Jesus up very high so that we all had to reach up to light our candles. I guess these people we stood for, even in Jesus' time, had to stretch quite a bit to get his ideas, too."

It is another year. The children have gathered for their first assembly after their summer vacations. They are eager to tell where they have been. They seem to have visited all parts of this great country. One describes Niagara Falls, one the Carlsbad Caverns, one the geysers at Yellowstone. Those who have not traveled so far tell of good times at camp, on farms, on beach picnics. They sing "America the Beautiful," a song so full of symbolic language it repays much study for interpretation, but the children know it from school training and sing it heartily. They join in a litany made from their experiences:

Litany: God, you have made a wonderful world!

In the summer when we have no school we can travel and see more of it. For the lakes and seashore places where we have fun swimming, and in boats, we thank you.

[*Refrain* (sung):] *We thank you, O God.*

For the woods and summer camping places, and for hills to climb,

[*Refrain:*] *We thank you, O God.*

For purple mountain peaks and tall pines; for rivers winding between canyon walls, for desert sands that look as if an artist had painted them; for geysers that spring up from the ground, and water falling over rocky ledges,

[*Refrain:*] *We thank you, O God.*

For caves and caverns where the dripping water has formed fairylands of beauty; for trees that are filled with golden fruit, and for all the sights we see from sea to shining sea,

[*Refrain:*] *We thank you, O God.*

60

"The Angelus" and the seven-branch candlestick are again on the platform. The man and woman in the picture are also thanking God, the children think, but not for blessings to America. They live in another country. This brings to the children's minds what they have heard of the suffering through war, and reminders of the potential "gardens" they sent in packets of seeds to Poland, Japan and Austria.

They name over the many blessings for which we in America can be thankful, for which they could light the candles each Sunday. A child goes to the platform to take the taper, and repeats what his candle shall stand for. "Families" come first, then "Homes" and "Seeds for food"; and "Hospitals"; then "That our town wasn't torn up by war," "That we can go to our own churches"; and then— "For freedom."

There are many more hands raised, but the candles are all lighted. Someone says, "There aren't enough candles for our ideas," and another, "We'll have to get more candles, we didn't mention schools."

In the department's teacher-supervisor conferences it was decided to do some interpreting of "America the Beautiful." Already the song had started one class on the study of what makes a good country. The teachers felt that there was danger of smugness in too much emphasis on what one can be thankful for, living in America. It is in truth a land of beauty and of plenty; but we are indebted to its heroes and patriots who have freed and cleared and peopled it. The prayer at the end of each stanza of the hymn makes one conscious of the need for spiritual greatness; of the weaknesses which threaten the land; of the responsibility that attends privilege.

The weaknesses are the weaknesses of those who sing

the hymn, who ourselves need a truer sense of values, a clearer vision of where we want to go and what it involves in human relationships to get there. But "brotherhood," "freedom," "flaw," "soul," "law," "thy gold refine," "gain divine," "alabaster cities . . . undimmed by human tears," while carrying a world of meaning to adults, with a whole panorama of pictures, mean little to children. The church school has an opportunity, throughout a year of services and class experiences, to fill at least some of those word symbols with feeling and with meanings.

In the class mentioned there was a listing on the board of what makes a good country. It was added to from time to time. Our own country—its homes, what the children knew of its institutions, its privileged and underprivileged groups—was measured by the listing, and some of the words in the song became clearer. Early in the study the class thought of laws which would be good for everybody and considered how it was that laws could make people "free" when liberty suggested freedom to do as one pleased.

In the departmental service, when the candles were lighted, there would follow conversations or meditations on parts of the hymn, e.g.:

It is a big country to be thankful for. It has wood and stone and precious metals to build and furnish homes and factories. It has farms and gardens which can produce food enough for all. . . . But is that all that makes a country good to live in, that *you and I* have enough to eat, that our homes and cities were not destroyed by war, that we have hospitals and churches and schools? Suppose somebody from another country came over here to live. Let's think what else would be needed to make him think he would be happy here. . . .

What picture comes to your mind when you hear the word *crown*? . . . In the prayer at the end of the first verse of the song we ask for something special to be added to all the wonderful things our country already has. It is as if the good things named were no more than any man might have, and putting a special crown on them made the man more kingly: "*Crown* thy good with brotherhood"; but how can we go about making brotherhood a part of our country? . . .

Let's sit quietly and think more about our country today. We love it and are proud of it. We like to hear stories of how it began and how it grew to be a great nation. We don't like to hear or think of anything that is wrong about it. When there is something wrong about a beautiful thing, we say there is a flaw in it. We don't like to think there are flaws in our country. That would mean that there is something wrong with us, or the way we act toward each other, for a country is made up of its people. Have you any ideas about what each one of us could try to do to make our part of the country a good part? . . .

A Prayer (after one of these meditative periods, or after a story of friends of Jesus who might ask questions like those indicated, or who, being perplexed by the multiplicity of laws they must follow, ask him to give them one inclusive rule):

God, who hast made us and put us here in a world with many others, may we learn how to live together happily; Help us to remember the rule about treating others as we wish to be treated ourselves. Help us to make our part of our home and of our country happy. Amen.

(The Golden Rule is set to a bit of Oratorio music on page 232 and can be sung after a prayer, or in a litany.)

Stories of those who have worked to make a better country are many, from those one knows of people in the community, to national figures like Jane Addams. A *Cheerful Cherub* verse called "Stained Glass Windows," by Rebecca McCann, viz.,

Stained glass windows make the light
Like songs of beauty from the sun.
Life could shine through us like that,
You, and me, and everyone

caused one boy to observe, after hearing the story of Jane Addams, "She was just like a window for all those people, she let the light shine through."

A THANKSGIVING LITANY (made from ideas given in departmental services, with refrain set to music by a second-grade class. Music on page 231.)

[Refrain:] *For thy helpers everywhere, we thank thee, O God.*

For all the people who have worked to make this a good country,

[*Refrain*]

For the Pilgrim Fathers who wanted it to be a place where everyone would be free to worship in their own way,

[*Refrain*]

For the Indians who taught them how to plant corn, and gave them turkey for their first Thanksgiving,

[*Refrain*]

For George Washington who was the first president, and who worked hard to make this a good country,

[*Refrain*]

For people like Jane Addams who help strangers feel at home and teach them to be happy and useful in their new country,

[*Refrain*]

For people like Mr. and Mrs. Edmonds who build houses where people from different countries can live together and get to know each other so they won't seem so different,

[*Refrain*]

For mothers and fathers who teach children to play together without quarreling, and for children and grown people who try to do to others what they would like others do to them,

[*Refrain*, ending with Amen.]

"DID JESUS SAY ANYTHING ABOUT A GOOD COUNTRY?"

In the class which was thinking about what makes a good country, "power" had been listed as one of the essentials. The story of the change Jesus' friendship wrought in Zacchaeus, however, and a poem read in class had raised some questions. The poem had begun:

> The brightest gleam that ever shone
> Across the dark world's night
> Was not reflected from the throne
> Of selfishness and might.[2]

The children were hearing also about St. Francis whose "power" was certainly not the kind the listing suggested.

("Jesus and St. Francis were alike in some ways," Arden said. "He probably got a lot of his ideas from Jesus." The teacher suggested that even today that was true, that perhaps that was what Phillips Brooks was thinking when he wrote his song.)

All this was in the background of their planning for another Christmas candle-lighting service for which they were already making candles, and for a poem of their own along the same lines. In the service, they decided, they would stand in a circle around one child who would hold a tall, white, lighted candle. The first child with a bayberry candle would light his from the white one, the second from the first, and so on, each child telling what his candle

[2] By Clarence Flynn. See p. 221 for entire poem.

stood for. Since the lights would stand for ideas and the way ideas travel from one person or group to another, the central one, Donald said, must represent someone whose ideas were very important.

The service which tried to take cognizance of Donald's question about Jesus and a good country invited the children to share their favorite stories of Jesus. Several pictures helped to illustrate the leader's talk.

Leader: Let's tell one another some of the stories about Jesus which we like best. (In each the leader pointed up the values Jesus' act brought out as over against what the populace might consider values.)

Talk: Sometimes we wonder where Jesus learned what he taught. Where do you learn what you know? (Answers.)

Some things Jesus learned from his father and mother, and from living with his sisters and brothers. (Picture of the boy Jesus in his home.) Some he learned in his school. His school was in the synagogue, a kind of church. (Picture.)

He learned the laws written down in the books of his people. There were big, important laws, like the one about not working on the Sabbath day, and those about cleanliness; and then many little ones to explain what the big ones meant.

For instance, you couldn't help anyone in trouble on the Sabbath day, if it meant that you had to work. You couldn't pick a bit of fruit if you were hungry, for that would be called work. It was the same about keeping clean. There were any number of rules about what you should eat to be "clean," and how you should wash your hands before eating, and just how to let the water run down to your wrists. Jesus had to learn rules like these in his synagogue school.

But there was another way he learned. (Picture: "Hilltop in Nazareth.") What do you think the boy is doing here? (After responses.) I think he often did what the boy seems to be doing here. And I think he thought about God a great

66

deal, talking to him, maybe, in his thoughts, maybe out loud; and listening to the thoughts that God might give him.

He seemed to learn new wisdom wherever he was; so much new wisdom that after a while he was making new rules for himself and for other people. They were all about getting along happily together, as in a big loving family, treating one another as each one would like to be treated himself, and all the time keeping close to God and trying to know his ways.

We have been thinking about countries—good countries —what makes a good country. Some say "Good laws; the right kind of rules."

But there were hundreds of laws in the country where Jesus lived, and still people weren't happy because of them. (Incident of sick woman healed on Sabbath, criticism, and Jesus' rebuke.)

So there were laws, but not good ones if people's needs and feelings were forgotten. Jesus thought that people were more important than laws.

You may have wondered if Jesus ever said anything about what makes a good country. In a way he did, but he didn't call it a country. He talked about a kingdom. There were more kings then, and people were used to that word. He talked about the kingdom of heaven. But where do you suppose he said the kingdom of heaven was? . . . It was not in the sky. It was not on any map.

He said the kingdom of heaven is in you!

He said people—like us—could bring it about if they wished for it hard enough; it could be right here on earth— now.

You see the kingdom of heaven is a kind of symbol. It *stands for* a kind of life, a way of thinking, a way of feeling. If people felt ugly, or mean or hateful, and didn't care what happened to others, then the kingdom of heaven would be far off. If they felt kind and friendly and cared what happened to others as much as what happened to themselves, then the kingdom of heaven would be right there!

Could you say that about a good country, then? If people are ugly and mean and don't care about what happens to their neighbors, how could it be a good country? But if they are friendly and kind and do care about what happens to others as much as what happens to themselves, why, it would be like the kingdom of heaven!

A PRAYER TO FOLLOW SUCH A TALK

Our Father who art in heaven, may thy kingdom "come true" in us; may thy work be done everywhere on earth as it is in the kingdom of heaven. May we have good feelings in us. May we always care what happens to other people, as Jesus did. Amen.

IV

Prayer Patterns
In the Primary Department

"I got a sled for Christmas," six-year-old Freddie reported on a snowy Sunday morning, "and I prayed to have it snow so I could slide."

"You did?" responded the teacher, hunting for a good snow song. "Well, your prayer was answered, wasn't it?"

For the teacher it was merely a conventional reply, given without thought. For the child, however, it was an encouragement to his own belief that he had only to pray for a favor and a benign Providence would grant it. Adults often thus unconsciously confirm in children concepts which become stumbling blocks in the development of a rational faith.

The teacher's slip led to more thought in her department on children's prayer patterns. How were they formed? Did the voiced prayers of adult leaders, or their manner of speaking of God, tend to give them shape? And was that shape consistent with what the children were learning, even in the early grades in school, through their experiments in "science," about the kind of world they live in?

Surely prayers should be based on assumptions which would not need to be revised, but which would increase in significance with growing experience.

That God operates in an orderly universe, through known or *discoverable* laws; that he may be seen in all creative and regenerative processes, both in nature and in man; and that, being Spirit he responds to prayers of the spirit—such assumptions would take prayer out of the realm of magic and suggest ways of praying which can be effective in a world operated through law.

In order, then, to lead Freddie and his group from "prayers for snow" to a better understanding of the way prayer can function in such a world, a series of services of worship was planned. Assumptions and aims implicit in the materials shared here are suggested in the titles.

I

"Teach Us To Pray Aright"

Setting: Picture on easel of people in attitude of prayer.

A Verse to Precede Meditation:

> This is a special place to which we come,
> For here we think of special things to say;
> Some make us happy, and we want to sing,
> Some make us thoughtful, and we want to pray.

Invitation to think of happy experiences which have come to the children recently, and to sing a song of joy. Verse above is repeated.

Meditation and Prayer (conducted slowly, with pauses between thoughts): God, you have made a world full of wonder and beauty and reasons for being glad and wanting to sing . . . But we are not always glad . . . We think, "If we had this, or that, we should be happy." "If only it would snow, or the sun would shine!" "If only we were rich, or we could have our own way!" And because we think of you as great, and wanting us to be happy, we sometimes think, if we pray, you will make things so . . . Great, wise, loving

70

Father of our spirits, teach us to understand your ways. Creator of worlds, make us to know the laws for this world in which you have brought us. Amen.

Conversation about Prayer (first about the people in the picture, what they are doing; if they are praying, what their prayers might be, considering the background. Then, why people pray. Are there different kinds of prayers? Do the children themselves pray? What about?):

(The responses will probably furnish a basis for thoughtful discussions and comparisons. Clark, for instance, declared he could make God do whatever he wished. He wanted company at supper that night, and he would write a nice prayer. Then God would have to do something he wanted. The others protested that you couldn't "boss God," but Clark was unconvinced. He spent the rest of the morning (one and a half hours) sitting by himself, producing a poetic prayer, in the course of which he forgot his original motive.

(Freddie told about his prayer for snow, and how it was "answered," but was at once met with, "Supposing someone else prayed to have a pleasant day?" Freddie had no immediate answer. Then Nielson said he wanted to have the radio keep going the other night—anyway until he went to sleep—so he prayed that it would, even though there was something wrong with the battery so it had stopped working. But this prayer was challenged as the other had been. Suppose, one child said, someone else wanted to go to sleep, and prayed to have it *stop*? Nielson assured the questioner that it was all right, the radio would have played very softly! But suppose it *had* disturbed somebody, who prayed for it to stop, how could God answer both prayers?

(Here Freddie, evidently finding a satisfactory solution to the question posed about his own petition, suggested that if one of the pray-ers was good, and one bad, God would discriminate that way.

71

(The leader was reminded of a prayer she had once made when she was a little girl. She would tell the children about it, and they could decide whether it was like Nielson's in any way, and whether it was a good prayer or a bad one.)

Leader's Reminiscence:

The little girl lived in the East, but her father was traveling in the West. When she wanted to ask him something, she wrote him a letter. It took three days for a letter to reach him.

The little girl wanted to go to dancing school; all her friends were joining the class, and talking about it. But it cost five dollars to join, and, of course, the little girl did not have five dollars. She sat down at her desk and wrote her father just how it was.

The next morning she came down the stairs with an excited, "expecting" feeling, as she held on to the banister because her eyes were squeezed tightly shut. She was praying. This was her prayer:

"Please, God, let there be a letter from my father in the mailbox, and let there be five dollars in it so I can go to dancing school!"

(The children who listened to the story all saw the foolishness of this prayer, but for different reasons.)

"He couldn't do it so quick: there weren't any airplanes in those days."

"No, it might have got stuck in the mud anyway, and not been on time." (Stagecoach era, evidently.)

"Maybe he was poor and couldn't send you the five dollars."

"Maybe he wanted the five dollars for something else."

"Maybe he didn't think she ought to have dancing lessons."

"Anyway, if it took three days to have a letter come, there wasn't time for it to be there that day."

Orrin had been doing some advanced figuring for a six-

72

year-old. "No," he agreed with Jimmy, "and it would take three days for a letter to get out there in the first place. That would make six days. *You could have prayed that you might get the five dollars in six days!*"

Charlotte, in the third grade, declared with emphasis, "It was a silly prayer: just like praying for the night to be short. It couldn't be any shorter than it is."

It *was* a silly prayer. It ignored too much which even this group knew about the world. You couldn't change night into day by praying. Day follows night according to a changeless law, operating in cycles of twenty-four hours.

(The leader asked what other laws of nature the children knew about. If she held up a glass of milk, and loosened her hold, what would happen? The children knew, there was the law of gravity.)

"But supposing I prayed, 'Please God, don't let this glass fall and the milk spill'?"

"It wouldn't make any difference," they declared. "The glass would have to fall and the milk spill."

"Then would my prayer be something like the little girl's prayer, and something like Nielson's? If a radio is out of order will a prayer to God make it work?"

(Nielson sat back in his chair. "Well, anyway," he said fatalistically, "I prayed it!")

"We often make prayers that would be hard for God to answer," the leader said, "like some we have talked about today. Everybody has to learn how to pray. Even grown people keep learning more and more about what makes a good prayer. We can all learn.

"While the music is playing, let's look again at the people in the picture, and imagine what their prayers might be."

Music

Prayer (introduced as parts of prayers made by people long ago, in the Bible, and which we still use today):

73

Open thou mine eyes, that I may behold
Wondrous things out of thy law. . . .
Give me understanding,
And I shall keep thy law. Amen.

II

PRAYER AND UNIVERSAL LAW

(Outline of talk given to Freddie's department by the school psychologist who had heard their discussion the week before:)

Imagine living in a time when the cavemen lived, when no one knew about science, nature, how things happen. Imagine how worried they'd be as the days grew shorter, and the sun stayed hidden longer, and the air grew cooler. Some thought the sun had died. They thought someone must have thought first of there *being* a sun, so they would pray to that god, "Oh, bring us back the sun! It means life and heat; we will do anything for you if you will bring us back the sun!" But the days would keep growing colder in spite of their prayers.

Then spring would come—warm weather; green grass; flowers; new life everywhere; gladness and festivities like our Easter rejoicing.

It was a long time before people realized that the sun did not rise, nor the rains come because of the whims of a god or the prayers of people, but *because of a law* which is one of many which regulate what happens in the skies and all the world of nature.

Conversation: Children and leader took time to think of consequences if they tried to depend on some law of nature like day following night, or water running down hill, and found it dependable only part of the time.

Psychologist's Talk Continued (to introduce idea of laws of

74

growth and for "getting along," and for "living together"—
for *people*):

At last men discovered there were laws for people, too.
If they acted in certain ways, certain results followed. It was
as if the Creator had thought, "I will put my law within
them, writing it on their hearts" (Moffatt). There were laws
for growing, laws for getting along with one another, laws
of kindness, laws of friendliness. If a law was broken, dis-
comfort or unhappiness followed. Co-operating with the law
gave a feeling of satisfaction, happier results. (Children's
illustrations, from parental displeasure to uncomfortable
feelings.)

So in time people learned to pray, instead of "Send us
rain," or "Send us sun," or "Hurry the growth of our plants,"
or *"Make me have lots of friends whether I treat them well or
not"*: "God, give me understanding, And I shall keep thy
law" (A.S.V.).

A Litany to Follow Talk:
> O God, whose laws will never change,
> We thank you for these things we know:
> That after rain the sun will shine,
> That after darkness, daylight comes,
> That winter always brings the spring
> For sap to flow, and seeds to grow.[1]

[*Response* (*sung*):] *We thank you, O God.*

> We thank you for the mind that plans
> To keep such order in the world.

[*Response:*] *We thank you, O God.*

> We thank you that for *each of us*
> Are laws to help us live and grow,
> And be what we were meant to be;
> And when we break a law of life

[1] From *Children's Worship in the Church School.*

75

That things go wrong;
But when we learn to follow it,
We work with you,
And grow
As you would have us grow.

[*Response:*] *We thank you, O God. Amen.*

Song: "Lord of the Sunlight" by Isabel Fiske Conant

Lord of the sunlight
Lord of the starlight,
Lord of the seasons, help me to know
How best to love thee,
How best to serve thee
Mid summer's flowers or winter's snow.

III

God Depends on the Love and Efforts of People

A Song of Joy: "Glad That I Live Am I."

An Older Song (from the Bible): "Thou hast put gladness into my heart."

Prayerful Meditation (conducted slowly, with pauses between sentences for reflection): God has put gladness into our hearts, too. We are glad for this beautiful sunny day, and all the happy things we may find to do in it . . . We are glad for our friends . . . We are glad for all the love that we have, and give . . .

There is sadness, too . . . Everybody is not happy . . . No one is happy all the time . . . Sometimes we understand the reasons. Perhaps people are hungry. Perhaps they are cold. Perhaps they have no friends to bring them happiness . . . Perhaps a friend has hurt another by something he said or did . . .

Sometimes we pray, "God bless everyone and make them happy," as if God could do that without our help.

O God, may we learn more and more how to put gladness into the hearts of others. Amen.

76

Recall of Discussions in the last two Sundays of different kinds of prayers, and why God cannot answer some.

Story (introduced as about a little boy who learned something new about how some prayers are answered): Little Trot.[2]

Story Outline:

Trot is making sand castles on the beach when his nurse comes from house with a roll, his mid-morning lunch. He is eating it when a ragged boy comes down the beach. Trot swallows the last bit of roll, asks boy if he has had his lunch. Finds there was no lunch. Trot suggests his asking God to send him some, but boy doesn't know anything about God. Trot explains that God gives Trot and his family everything they need, and they pray every night. Tells boy what to say asking God to send him lunch, even to suggesting safe place in rock-cave to deposit it. Boy promises to pray and return next day. In morning Trot goes to cave to make sure prayer has been answered. Nothing there. He wonders. Sees nurse coming with his roll. Runs to take it and puts it in cave just as ragged boy arrives. Trot watches him hungrily eat his roll. It was good, but boy says, "God didn't put it there, you did. I saw you." Trot puzzled, but says he thinks God must need people to help him sometimes. His father plants garden, but doesn't make it grow. His mother has to feed the chickens—"and I think he wanted me to help him with that roll." Boy says, "Oh! Shall I pray for one tomorrow?" Trot answers, "Yes," and when boy has gone, says to nurse, "Please bring two rolls tomorrow."

Offering (relating it to people the children know working in settlements, camps, hospitals, etc., who are helping God, working with him, doing what God could not do alone).

Song: "Lord of the Sunlight."

[2] Adapted from Lichtenberger's book, *Mon Petit Trot*. Translated by Elizabeth Colson. Found in *A Second Primary Book in Religion*, O. P. Colson, and in various courses for Primary children.

Wishes That Become Prayers

Every school has interests in institutions in the community, and there is usually a story about the beginnings of one of these which would be of more interest than the one used with the department being described. A first grade had visited a day nursery near by, made applesauce for one of the children's lunches, were bringing money for orange juice, and toys for their amusement. A second grade had had a visit from the director of the Church of All Nations who told the story of the Settlement's beginnings.

A third grade had a friend who directed a convalescent home for crippled children. The class had just had a delightful experience entertaining several of the little "convalescents," who had come to the church in their casts, slings and braces, and at once became eager participants in the class work. They had had no self-consciousness or sense of handicap. Their pride in their braces and their matter-of-fact willingness to tell just what conditions were being corrected by treatment banished pity on the part of their hosts and aroused, instead, admiration for the knowledge and skill of scientists, doctors and nurses.

The service which followed that experience has value only as it suggests a framework for group thinking on the manner in which we may make it possible for God to answer some of our prayers. Even children's concern, if it is deep enough, may bring about the blessings they pray for, as it opens the way for God's laws to operate.

Prayerful Music (listened to as children thought what "prayers" the music might be trying to express, followed by *gay, joyful* music, as children try also to catch this mood).

78

A Poem to Read: "Something Right Inside Me"[3] (which thanks God for strength to "run and jump and play," while the last stanza asks God to make all children "healthy and strong like me, to run and jump and play").

Leader: It would be a happy thing if just by asking God to make all children well and strong and gay they could become so. Do you think that could happen? What do babies need to have, to grow up into well, strong children? (Answers.) Could God provide this without people?

It would be fine if, just by wishing, all the children in the city could have good places to play and clubs to join where lonely ones could make friends. But what has to happen first, before there can be Neighborhood Houses like the Church of All Nations? (Answers.)

Wishing and praying are a little different. In fairy stories when a fairy grants three wishes to a child, we're not surprised at all when they come true suddenly, and without any effort on the child's part. In the world of fairies and magic anything may happen. But we know that the world of fairies and magic is not real; it is only a play world.

Prayers are more than wishes for something magical to happen. When we pray, we are thinking of this world, the real world we live in. We remember how God works in this real world; that he has special ways, according to laws, and we can study his ways and know how to work with him.

Sometimes wishes turn into prayers. People begin by wishing something that seems impossible. But they wish so hard that they try to find out ways to make it possible. They pray to God to help them find more and more ways to make it possible. Thoughts come to them, new ideas for work to make the wish come true. Strength comes to do the work. All the time they may keep on praying to be sure of working in the right way. I know a story about somebody's wishes that turned into a whole hospital! (Story followed of founder of

[3] From *The Children's Kingdom* by Gwendolyn Watts. Found also in *Children's Worship in the Church School.*

convalescent hospital which started with "Sister Sarah" working in a crippled children's home in Philadelphia, because she wished to help children to be well; taking three of her little patients to Brooklyn where a house had been offered her, and working and wishing and praying until she had not only founded a hospital in the city, but a big sunny Home in the country, where hundreds of happy children have lived, gone to their own school, learned to play musical instruments, and make things with their hands; and most important, learned to use bones and muscles that they could not use before.)

Song: "Glad Let Us Be for People" (second and third or fourth stanzas, see page 234).

Meditation: Let us think of the *wishes* we would make for children who are sick or crippled . . . Now let us think of some of the *work* which must be done if such wishes come true . . . Now let us think *if there is any part of that work we could do ourselves.*

Let us think of little children who are not ill, but whose mothers work all day and need a place to leave them where they will be cared for. What shall we wish for them? . . . Let us think what day nurseries need and what the children in them would like . . . Let us think of something we could do to help a little bit toward such a need . . .

Now let us think of children in our city who need friends and places to play. Some have just moved here and are lonely. Some can't even speak our language. Some live near us and go to our schools . . .

("Prob'ly there are lots of Japanese and German and Italian children here right now that want friends," Walter suggested.)

If we could have our wish, what would we wish for them? . . .

And now let's think of something we can do ourselves to make the wish come true . . .

80

Prayer: May our wishes turn into prayers, O God, and our prayers into ways of working with you. Amen.

Song: "Lord, I want to be more loving in my heart."

V

"You Pray for What You Can't Buy"

TWO STORIES

The Short Story, which introduces the longer one:

Margaret watched her father get ready to go to the office. "I prayed for some roller skates," said Margaret. "Do you pray for things, Daddy?"

"Yes, I pray," answered her father, "I pray every day."

Margaret wondered what big people like her father would want: an automobile? A bicycle? A new suit? A new house?

As her father said "No" to all of these, she asked, puzzled, "Then what *do* you pray for, Daddy?"

"Well," her father said, "I pray that I'll have a good day, that I'll have a clear head and do good thinking; and that if things go wrong I won't lose my temper. I pray that I'll try to understand the people I'm working with, and that I'll be kind."

Margaret was quiet a moment. These things weren't a bit like roller skates or bicycles. Then she said, "Oh, I see, *you pray for what you can't buy in stores.*"

The Long Story: How Harold Helped.[4]

Outline Notes: Harold was sulking. No, he wouldn't go to the concert. Instead he went to his room and shut the door. His mother, gifted Negro singer, had just told him something. He couldn't bear to think of it. Already, she could sing better than anyone in the world: why should she think she had to go abroad and study all those months? Even if her teacher had told her that she had "a great gift to give to the

[4] Outlined and slightly adapted from a story by Annie Sills Brooks.

world," and a "message from their race to other races," why did she have to give it, if it meant being away from him all that time?

He hears the car door slam. His father and mother have left for the concert.

He decides after all to go, on foot . . . sits high up in balcony; forgets everything but joy in mother's singing. It is always like this. He leaves before the rest, is reading when parents come home. He can talk with his mother now. They sit on the couch, her arm around him. Mother saw him at the concert—it helped her sing better. Says she doesn't want to leave Harold and his father—will stay if they say so, but explains: "Sometimes people of one race do not understand those of another. Music is one of the things that make them understand. Perhaps my music could do this."

Father and son together decide she ought to go. Mother finds boarding school for Harold, and promises to come home any time he writes her that he needs her. He says good-by bravely.

Unhappy at school; boys are mean to new boy. Harold on point of writing mother several times to come home, and one day, when boys put him on a box and make him make a speech, is so angry he rushes to his room and does write. On way to post office head of the school with visitor calls him: "Oh, Harold! Here is a gentleman who knows your mother, would like to meet you." Visitor says, "I saw your mother off on her ship . . . she is a great artist . . . it was hard for her to leave you . . . said she never could at the last if you had not been so brave . . said it was helping her to be brave."

Harold goes on, biting his lips. Fists clenched in pockets, prays, "O God, help me to be as brave as my mother thinks I am!" Takes letter from pocket, tears it up, puts scraps in trash basket on street.

Things easier after that. Writes mother of his good marks, counts the weeks before her return. Then Harold has an accident; breaks leg, is hospitalized when letter comes from abroad. Mother's teacher wants her to extend time there three months. Are her "men-folk" willing? Oh, no! Harold needs her! She said she would come if he needed her, and now he really does. She would want to be there if she knew her boy was in the hospital. He had been living for her return—only two weeks away. Harold's father wants her back, too, but wants to help her get the proper training. He agrees that if she knew Harold had had an accident she would come flying home, but it is left up to Harold to decide whether to tell her or not. It must be as hard for her to stay away from them as it is for them not to have her, father says, but evidently she thinks it important in giving her "message" to stay, or she would not have written them.

Again Harold pushes back the tears and decides not to write. Makes a new calendar and marks off the days.

One evening largest auditorium in the city is filled to hear a great singer. Harold this time in front row with father. All around them people not of their race, but eager for concert to begin. As soon as mother begins to sing Harold knows something is in her voice that was not there before she went away. Great ovation. When she sings "Home, Sweet Home" as last encore, tears are in everyone's eyes. She seems to be telling them all how she has missed her home, how she loves it. They all understand, for they have homes, too, and feel the same way about theirs. Harold is glad he tried so hard to be brave. She looks straight at him when she sings. Her smile at the end seems to say, "You helped me give this message."

VI

"Lord, Show Me One Good Thing That I Can Do" [5]

Quiet Music, ending with air of refrain of "Portuguese Hymn" and singing of "Call to Worship," "Come, Oh Come, Let Us Worship."

Poem:

> To this quiet place of worship
> We have come from work-day things,

[5] Verses are from *As Children Worship*; both made from thoughts of children.

Pausing for a while and waiting
For the thoughts that quiet brings.

Silence

Directed Meditation: Let us remember why we come here each
Sunday morning:

To sing, and to make friends;
To think, and to have stories,
To work, and play, and learn;
To have a restful time,
Thinking, in the silence,
About ourselves and God.

Leader (after Silence): There is a part of ourselves which we
cannot see, and cannot touch, yet we know it is there. It is
what makes you *you*, and me *me*. It is the part that feels, and
thinks, and wishes. Even without words we can pray and
God can understand. And without words he can speak to us
and we can understand.

I am going to tell you about somebody who prayed a
prayer, with words, and how the answer came with no
words at all, and how it was understood.

When the country of China was invaded by her enemy
early in a war, a young man whom his friends called Bill
was principal of a high school. It was a North American
missionary school, and he and his teachers were teaching
what they thought the boys and girls ought to know. But
the enemy soldiers had different ideas and said to Bill, "You
must teach our ideas or we will shoot you."

Now Bill didn't want to be shot, and he wouldn't teach
what he was told to teach, so he slipped out of the city one
night and started to walk across China to a place six hundred miles away. There was another school, with other
American teachers there, but it was in a part of the
country strange to Bill, and it took him a long time to reach
it. He had no friends on the way, and part of the time he
was lonely, and part of the time terribly unhappy.

84

He found himself near the battle front and saw sights that made him feel like weeping. There were very few doctors where the men in China were fighting, only one, perhaps for thousands and thousands of men. Bill kept seeing wounded soldiers who needed care badly, and many who were too hurt to get food for themselves. Everywhere he looked was misery, and there was he, Bill, knowing nobody, and unable to do anything to help.

That was when Bill prayed. All day he went up and down among the strange and sad sights, praying one prayer: "O God, show me one good thing that I can do! *God, show me one good thing that I can do!*"

Finally an idea came to him, and he said to the first person he met, "Will you be a friend to the wounded soldiers?"

The first person was a very poor farmer. All he had was a patch of garden and two hens. A good hen in America will lay about two hundred eggs a year, but this Chinese hen would probably not give the farmer in the whole year more than sixty. The farmer said he was poor and could not do anything, but Bill did not give up. "Won't you give one egg a week to a soldier," he asked, "and will you go and find this soldier and cook it and feed it to him?" and the farmer said he would.

That was a small beginning, but Bill did not stop there. He asked the next person, and the next, until the idea spread from one to another, and another. No one had much money, but they could all promise to do one thing for one soldier every week, and sometimes more. Bill gave to each helper a button which said, "I am a Friend of the Wounded Soldiers," and people, seeing the button, would ask about it, and then become helpers, too.

In just one month that small beginning grew to a society with two million members. Two million friends for wounded soldiers from one man's prayer![6]

[6] This story was told by Dr. James Endicott, at that time secretary of the New Life Movement in China. He was formerly a missionary of the United Church of Canada.

Prayer: God, we are glad there are people like Bill in the world who want so much to be of use, and make things better than they are that they will pray and pray, "Show me one good thing that I can do!" We are thankful that you could speak to him in his thoughts, and that he could understand you. Make us ready to speak to you, God, and to listen to the thoughts you send us. Amen.

Song: "Lord, I want to be a Christian in my heart."

VII

THE MAN WHO TALKED WITH FLOWERS: THREE PICTURES

Rackham Holt's book, *George Washington Carver* (Doubleday), contains material for many stories, both for worship and class study. The record of this deeply religious man who talked intimately with God and sought constantly to understand the world He created is peculiarly fitting for use in our church schools. A small book, by Glenn Clark, published earlier is called *The Man Who Talked with Flowers* (Macalester Park Publishing Co.). The following talk acknowledges indebtedness to both these works.

The name of the man we are going to think about today is George Washington Carver. A friend of his called him "The Man Who Talked with Flowers." Why do you suppose he talked with flowers, and how do you think he could understand their language? He did understand; he used to say they told him their secrets. What secrets do you think flowers could have? . . .

In the books that have been written about this man are stories which make pictures in my mind. The first picture is of a colored boy who has a patch of ground he calls his

86

secret garden. Into this garden he brings the sick plants of the neighbors, for they have learned that when their plants wither, George can usually make them well again. I see him looking long at a drooping stalk, touching it tenderly, *talking to it.* "What is the matter with you?" he asks, and waits, studying it. Then he nods his head, loosens the roots, packs new soil around it and puts it in a sunny spot. Then I see him scraping the earth. The ground is hard, for there has been a frost. He comes to a piece of bark, which he lifts away, and uncovers a warm hollow in the ground. He brings out from the hollow place a plant, and then another. "Did you keep good and warm where I put you to bed?" he asks; then, just as if he knew the plants could understand, explains, "I knew there'd be a frost last night, so I had to dig a warm place for you. The sun is out now, and you can stay out all day. The sun will help you grow."

The next picture has a sunrise in it. It is very early in the morning on a hillside. George has grown up now. He is a teacher. All these years he has been living with plants of many kinds, caring for them, asking them questions, learning the answers. He is asking questions now. He has a flower in his hand. "What are your secrets, little flower? Why did the Creator make you?" He sits down on a stump with the flower in his hand and looks and looks. Then he talks to God. He calls him Mr. Creator. He says, "Mr. Creator, why did you make *me?* What do you want me to do?" He waits, then gets up and starts down the hill as if he had a new idea.

The third picture shows him walking across some land. It is land on which hardly anything will grow. But peanuts are growing where he has planted them. He is glad, for the farmers all around that part of the country are very poor. They have almost starved, because nothing would grow. Now they can grow peanuts. Hundreds and hundreds of acres can grow peanuts where nothing grew well before.

But Dr. Carver's brow is puckered. He is thinking. After the people have eaten all the peanuts they want, what will the rest be good for? There must be some other uses for the peanut.

He pulls up a handful, goes back to his laboratory with the peanuts in his hand, and talks to God.

Those are some of the pictures of Dr. Carver I have in my mind. But the books tell a great deal more about him.

Sometimes Dr. Carver asked the plants for their secrets; often he asked questions of God. That was the way he prayed, and always he knew he would have an answer.

Dr. Carver used to tell how he talked to God one day about the peanut. He said, "I told the Creator I wanted to know all about the peanut. He said my mind was too small to know *all* about it, but he taught me how to take the peanut apart and put it together again."

What Dr. Carver meant was that in his laboratory he could analyze the peanuts and separate the oil, and the water and the gum, and the sugar, and lots of other different parts. After he had done that, Dr. Carver said God reminded him of certain laws of science. The laws showed him how the parts could be put together differently, and make other things besides peanuts.

So Dr. Carver began to experiment with the parts of the peanut. He made a kind of milk, for one thing, that has saved the lives of many babies. He made peanut butter and vinegar and soap and pickles, and sauce and rubber and buttermilk and cheese, and paper and ink and metal polish and a kind of oil which he rubbed on little children who had infantile paralysis and which made them feel better. Those are only a few of the uses he found for the peanut.

So there was plenty of reason for the farmers to plant their lands with peanuts!

The plants had told him their secrets, and God had answered his prayer, but neither the flowers nor the Creator had had to use words. "If you love them enough," Dr. Carver said, "they will tell you their secrets."

A Prayer: God of love, and Creator of worlds, open our eyes that *we* may behold wondrous things out of thy law. May we learn to pray better, to study your ways, and discover how to work with you. Father of our spirits, *what do you want us to do?* (Silence, ending with musical phrase.)

VIII

THE HANDS THAT HELPED A FRIEND

In most stories of prayer the interest is centered on the subject prayed for, and whether and how the prayer is answered. The story related of Albrecht Dürer's "Praying Hands" has another value. It does not tell us what the owner of those hands is praying for, but it suggests, like the hands themselves, a great spiritual need. It is entirely legendary, indeed at variance with what is recorded of the professional life and early success of this fifteenth century painter. It is, however, a legend greatly beloved, and, told to the children in one of its many adaptations, may give a deeper significance to prayer than they have yet grasped. It is the story of the sublimation of an unfulfilled desire; of the need of communion with God in the face of unanswered prayer.

The group which was earlier talking about prayer as a sort of magic formula showed by their responses to this story a different kind of appreciation of the function of prayer. As a little girl once said, "You pray for what you can't buy." The values the children mentioned here were spiritual values, which one "cannot buy." Their comments follow the story, which was introduced by a study of the picture, and "This is a story which is told about it."

THE PRAYING HANDS

There was once a boy named Albert who, from the time he was your age, was always drawing pictures. He drew them on scraps of paper, on school pads, and even on the margins of books. He was scolded for marking on the books, but his father would say proudly, "He will be able to make fine designs for us even before he is the usual age for apprentices. Soon I can take him into my shop."

Albert's father was a goldsmith. That meant he made dishes and jewelry of silver and gold. An apprentice was a boy who worked about the shop of a master, learning his trade as he worked and helped. Albert liked the drawing part—he liked making designs—but he was not nearly as interested in working in silver and gold as in ink and wood and paint. Left to himself he would draw pictures of people, and whenever he could, he would go to see the drawings and paintings that great artists had made.

He did go into his father's shop, and start to learn a goldsmith's trade as his father wished. After all, he must learn a trade, as all boys did, and begin soon to earn money. It was a large family to which Albert belonged, and his help was needed.

But he was unhappy. "I don't want to be doing this," he would say to himself. "I want to learn to draw and paint! I should be taking lessons from a master artist!" Such a plan would take him away from his father's shop, however, where he was needed.

At last his family, seeing his unhappiness, and really believing that if he could have the right instruction he might some day be a great artist, scraped together what they could to send him to the city where he could study. There he found a tiny room and set about finding work to pay for his food and rent.

He kept so busy he had no time to make friends, and he was often lonely. Every spare moment he gave to practicing drawing. At lunchtime he would sit at a table and draw the people around him; on Sundays he would sit in the park and watch people go by and try to sketch them from memory.

The story is told of his meeting one day a man who stopped to look at the picture Albert was drawing. "That is good," he said. "Are you studying with one of the masters?"

"No," Albert told him, "but I hope to be soon. The trouble is, I have no money for the lessons, and as fast as I earn any it goes for food and a room." He looked at the long slender fingers of the older man. "Are you an artist?" he asked.

"I should like to be," the older man said, as he sat down beside Albert. "All my life I have wanted to learn to paint, but my trouble is the same as yours. I have never yet had money enough to pay for lessons."

So they talked together. Each was glad to find a friend who understood his troubles, and before long they had hit upon a scheme to save money for each of them. They decided to live together and share the rent of one room.

Still neither one could save enough for the art lessons they each wanted so much. One day Albert's friend had an idea. "Look here," he said. "Why doesn't one of us do the earning and the other take lessons until he can paint and sell pictures? Then he can do the earning and the other can have his turn at lessons."

"A fine idea," said Albert. "You go first to the school, while I work."

But his friend would not have it that way. "No," he said, "I have a good job at a restaurant, where my meals don't cost anything. And besides, you already draw better than I do and will learn faster; you go first."

So it was settled. Albert went to his lessons each day and his friend went to work. His work in the restaurant was hard, for he washed the dishes and scrubbed the floors, and even the walks outside. His hands were in water so much that in the cold weather they would get frost-bitten and stiff, and pains would go up and down his arms. His hands got out of shape a little, and his joints were so swollen and stiff that it was hard to move his fingers. But he kept at it, happy in the thought that Albert was getting on well, and that his turn would come sometime. He did not mind the cracked nails, or the crook which came in his little finger.

At last one evening Albert came bounding up the stairs. "News! Great news!" he called out, as he burst into the room.

91

"My first sale! See!" holding out his hand. "Money enough for food and rent for weeks ahead. Now, my friend, your turn has come!" He was as excited and pleased as his friend that at last the other could have his chance.

The very next day the friend went to his first lesson. His hands trembled as he started to draw the first lines. The pencil would not go where he wanted it to go. Perhaps the paints would be better. But no, his hands still trembled, and his fingers could not grasp the brush. Perhaps tomorrow it would be better.

But though he tried the next day and the next, and for many days, he realized at last, sadly, that he had waited too long. His hands were too crippled to hold the brush; he could never be a painter. At first he tried not to let Albert know, but as time went on Albert had to know. His friend's disappointment sent a great pang of grief through Albert's heart.

"What can I do for him, who has done so much for me?" he kept asking himself. "Take care of him always, yes, he shall always share what I have. But the dearest wish of his life I cannot make come true!"

They had moved to a larger place now, and one day Albert came home unexpectedly to find the house very quiet. His friend must be out, he thought, stepping through a doorway. But his friend was not out. He was there. His eyes were closed, his hands were together. He was praying.

Albert looked at those hands: cracked nails, swollen and crooked joints, stiff wrists, but still an artist's hands. To him they were the most beautiful hands in the world.

Quietly he brought out his crayons and his pad. "I cannot give him back what he has lost," he said to himself, "but I can give to the world to keep forever the beauty of those hands."

So he made a picture of those hands as they were joined in prayer, and people for years and years have loved to look at it and think of the story back of it.

Conversation about the Story

"I wonder what the friend might have been praying?" the leader asked when this story was told to the Primary group.

"Maybe he was praying for his hands to get better," ventured one child, but the hopelessness of this was lifted as another spoke, as if he himself were the friend praying: *"Help me not to be sorry I did it."*

It was quiet a moment, then, *"Don't let me get mad that I can't paint,"* came from a third-grade boy; from a second-grade girl, *"Help him to be a great artist,"* and finally, from another: *"Help me to keep on loving him."*

"What do you think might be a good title for this picture?" the leader asked as she turned to the picture on the easel, and all these were given: The Crippled Hands; The Lovely Hands; The Hands That Helped a Friend; The Praying Hands; The Hands of Art; The Hands of Love; The Hands That Worked; The Working Hands; The Hands That Did So Much for Me.

Biographical Note on Albrecht Dürer

Albrecht Dürer, born in the latter half of the fifteenth century, was the son of a Hungarian goldsmith who had wandered to Bavaria and settled in Nürnberg, an art center, married the daughter of his employer, and raised a large family. Albert early showed marked artistic talent, and though valuable in his apprenticeship to his father, did not wish to be a goldsmith. The great artist Wohlgemuth lived on the same street, and agreed to take the boy into his studio and shop where he made his frames. Here Albert received his first instruction while helping the master in various ways. He became a master in his own right, rising to fame through his many drawings, woodcuts, copper engravings and paintings. It is not known how he happened to draw "The Praying Hands," or whose hands were portrayed, but the legends have long enhanced appreciation of the picture.

93

V

"Wondrous Things Out of Thy Law"

Open our eyes that we may behold
Wondrous things out of thy law.

It was a verse used often in the worship of the Primary
department, for although "our eyes" are constantly being
"opened" there have always been more marvels unfolding,
and new aspects of what was already familiar.

Virginia had sung a tune to the words, which increased
their use, for the verse now became a refrain for a litany.

It was a sort of "theme song" whose melody, even without the words, set the mood for a service of worship.

AN OUTSIDE SPEAKER ENRICHES THE SERVICE OF WORSHIP

George Washington Carver has always been one of the
school's favorite heroes. A second grade had given a play
about his early childhood. A third grade had a more am-
bitious one in preparation. (The first was to show the
kindness of the people who took him in as a child; the
second, his struggle and his contribution to the world.)
When the supervisor learned that a church school father,
who represented the firm from which its paints and crayons were ordered, had known Dr. Carver intimately, she
asked if he would tell the children about his experiences
with him.

In every community are individuals who can contribute

to children's appreciations of persons who work in harmony with the laws or "will" of God; who are a part of the answer to the prayer, *Thy will be done.*

This young man, Mr. Johnson, was particularly gifted. He made his whole audience feel the warm personality of Dr. Carver through his own affectionate admiration for him. He explained how when he was a student at "Georgia Tech" he was studying subjects quite different from what Dr. Carver's interest led him into—that of working with pigments. His brother was in the peanut business, and was one of those whom Dr. Carver called "his boys," as he himself became.

On an easel on the platform was a large photograph of Carver, which Mr. Johnson had taken and enlarged, and on the table were spread samples of Alabama soil, of different colors, a sweet potato, and many peanuts.

He told how, when he first met the great man, they "just liked each other," and the mutual affection continued until Dr. Carver's death. Mr. Johnson had many letters from him. Sometimes one would come every day, sometimes with a week's interval between them. He read a part of one of the letters. It began, "My beloved boy."

He made the group feel Dr. Carver's reverence for nature; one of his favorite verses from the Bible being "I will lift up mine eyes unto the hills, from whence cometh my help." This was literally true, for the clays and soil from the hills around held secrets for him which helped in discovering innumerable useful properties which could be joined with others to make new products. "His boys" would carry buckets to the hills and fill them with the soil. Dr. Carver would tell them, "Be careful how you carry that; there's treasure in the pail." And back in the laboratory they would analyze the soil and find the "treasure."

Another of Dr. Carver's favorite verses was, "The earth is the Lord's and the fulness thereof."

Mr. Johnson showed the children samples of the colored soil, and many paintings he had made because Dr. Carver had advised him to "play with color." He made his own paints from the different kinds of soil.

He told the group about some of the things Dr. Carver found out about the sweet potato, and before them he "took apart" a peanut and explained how, among other products, Dr. Carver had made paper from the shell, dye from the red skin over the nut, and butter and milk from the nut itself. He said he would give each child a peanut to take home and tell his parents about it.

The service that day was of course planned around Mr. Johnson's visit.

Quiet Music: Selected, then music for "Open Our Eyes That We May Behold."

Processional: "Hark to the Sound." For its lines:

> Praise Him for friends
> Who help us know
> Wonders of God
> The world may show.[1]

Songs: "Come, oh come, let us worship, sing unto the Lord with thanksgiving."

> "We thank thee, O God." For the lines:
> For showing the seeds how to press through the sod,
> And tell in their silence the wonders of God.[2]

Bible Verses: The earth is the Lord's and the fulness thereof,
The world, and they that dwell therein. . . .
Open mine eyes that I may behold
Wondrous things out of thy law. . . .

[1] From *As Children Worship.*
[2] From *Children's Worship in the Church School.*

96

I will lift up mine eyes unto the hills
From whence cometh my help.

Prayer Song: "Quiet our minds and our spirits."

Prayer (continued): God, we know that we have discovered only a small part of your wonders. The earth is full of them; the sea is full of them; the sky and air are full of them. They are there for us to discover and to use, and to share with one another. We thank you for all those who have tried to find out about your world and what you have put in it. We pray that we may grow up wanting to work with you to bring more food, more health, more beauty to people around us, as did the man we are going to hear about today.

Response: Music for "Thank You, God." Amen.

Mr. Johnson's Talk

Song: "Glad Let Us Be for People" (page 234).

Music while procession formed for the peanuts.
    (Note: No child was seen eating his. It was as though it was something new and precious.)

"WE CAN BUT WATCH AND WONDER"

It is fall, and the children arrive bearing autumn leaves and bits of plants gone to seed. In a first grade they tell of flocks of birds flying south, and the days growing shorter. Nature is following its age-old pattern. Man has no hand in these changes. "This is the Lord's doing," the Psalmist sang. The teacher repeats the words, adding, "we can but watch and wonder" (Moffatt).

One of the children makes a tune for the words, and the group shares it with the other first grade.

In this class a green and a red apple have been opened to find out what colors their respective seeds might be. A surprise—they look exactly alike! How did some know

97

they must turn into red apples, and some green? Here, too, one "can but watch and wonder." But the seeds will know, there must be rules for different kinds of seeds, as for the leaves in autumn, and for the south-bound birds, and the seeds and the leaves and the birds must know them, for they always act the same way.

In a second grade two children have visited the Planetarium. Two others have "star books" at home. They all talk learnedly about the planets, the North Star, and the changes in the sky at different seasons of the year. Here, too, are mysteries exciting curiosity and awe. The children talk about the night, how it always comes, and if you can't see the stars because of clouds, the stars are there just the same; and how one can be sure that day will come, because it always does. There are some things "that are always." We don't know how these things can be—does anybody know?

The interest of the different classes are brought together in the service of worship, and form the basis for a litany whose refrain quite naturally is the little song:

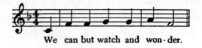
We can but watch and won-der.

The song of George MacDonald's is sung:

> The sun has gone down,
> And the moon's in the sky,
> But the sun will come up,
> And the moon will be laid by, etc.

and the story told of Alice Geer Kelsey's "The Constant Star."

The music supervisor decided to teach the song, "Maker of the Planets" (page 236), and as one second grade was working on family life and "getting along together," a service which took all these interests into account was planned.

After the Call to Worship, and a praise song had been sung, the first grades were invited to tell about their seeds, show their paintings of autumn, and their "rhythm" of departing birds. This was followed by

Meditation on the "Things that are always"

>Seeds—growing the same way each year
>Stars—in their courses
>Birds—returning south in fall

Musical Phrase (ending Silence).

Prayer: We thank you, God, for putting us in a world where we can depend on your ways. We have called your ways *laws,* and know you have given us minds to find out more and more about them. We pray, with the people of long ago:

>Open our eyes that we may behold
>Wondrous things out of thy law. Amen.

Introduction to Story:

It would be fine if we could depend on people as we can on stars and seeds. If God has laws for everything else he has created, people have asked, why not for us, too? And they have discovered some.

If seeds need soil and water and sun to grow, what do children need? . . . If they cannot have them, what will happen? . . . That is a kind of rule or law.

If there is a "law" within the birds, telling them when to fly south, and they do not obey that law, what happens? . . .

99

In the story I am going to tell, see if you think there is a law for people, too, which can be depended on, so that if it is obeyed, certain things follow, or if it is disobeyed, something else will follow.

Story: How Timothy Found His Place

Timothy was the very smallest of a large family of brothers and sisters. Because he was the youngest, no one thought what he did or said was important. "Timothy is so small," they would say, or "Timmy is so young." If he came in with the story of something he had seen in the woods or on the road they would say, "Run and wash your hands, Timmy," without listening to what he had to tell them. Or they might smile at one another and whisper, "He thinks he saw that. He's so little he doesn't know the difference."

Even though Timmy grew older each year, he was still so much younger than the rest that they felt that nothing he said or did counted. Everyone else in the family did count. Each one was important in some way, but Timmy seemed to have no place at all except to be the baby of the family. Whenever there was a special errand to be done one of the older children was asked to do it. "Timmy's too young," they would say, if they thought of him at all. They would say it when there was work to do and he wanted to help. They even said it when he wanted to give his mother a birthday present.

"You aren't old enough to have money of your own, you see," his brothers and sisters told him, "so you can't buy one. And you can't paint or draw or sew or build like Edward and Eve and Ethel and Henry, so how can you make her one?"

"I know something she would like," he said, "a sewing box that plays a little tune when you lift the lid to get the thread. I saw it in the village."

"Sewing boxes do not play tunes," replied big brother Nat.

"But this one did," answered Timothy eagerly. "It has a pretty tune. I heard it. The shop man was showing it to a lady."

100

"Really," one sister remarked to the others, "that child imagines the strangest things!"

"But I did not imagine it," Timothy protested. "Truly I saw it. If you will give me a silver piece I will walk to town and get it in time for the birthday celebration tonight. Then it will be partly my present because I found it."

The brothers and sisters smiled at one another. Not one of them believed there was a musical sewing box, but at last one of the brothers said, "Let us give Timothy the money and see what he will bring back. If it is a sewing box with tunes, we will believe him; if it is the silver piece we shall know he imagined it."

The others finally consented, and Timothy started to town, feeling for the first time really important in his family. He walked very fast, whistling happily, and holding tight to the large round silver piece in his pocket. He was so proud of his errand that when he saw Harold, a boy in the town whom he knew, he at once showed him the big coin and told what it was to buy.

"I am doing an errand, too," Harold said, "but see, my silver piece is larger than yours."

They compared the coins and put them back in their pockets.

"Let us go to the green for a drink," Timothy said. "I am thirsty from my long walk."

So they went to the green and drank from the fountain there. Then, because the green was smooth and soft, they tumbled about for a few minutes, turning somersaults and rolling over and over on the grass.

"Now I must go and buy the sewing box," said Timothy, "and hurry back for the celebration."

He left Harold and made his way to the store. There was the sewing box which he had seen. The shop man showed again how a little music box played when the cover was lifted, and Timothy, eagerly listening, put his hand in his pocket for his silver piece.

It was not there! Timothy was frightened, but not too

101

frightened to think. He remembered the somersaults on the green. It must have fallen from his pocket there. He ran back as fast as his legs could carry him, and searched through the grass. When a piece of silver shone up at him he seized it joyfully, but when he looked at it closely he saw that it was Harold's larger piece. If it had only been his! He searched on and on, but it was useless. Discouraged, he looked again at the coin in his hand and wished he could use it. But this coin was Harold's, and Harold must be as worried as he. He must take it to Harold's house at once, although it was at the other end of the town, and the afternoon was nearly gone.

It seemed a long, long way to Harold's, and when he had left the money at the door he turned, a tired little boy, toward home. His steps dragged, and he felt like crying. How could he go home late, with neither the sewing box nor his money? What should he say? And what would his brothers and sisters say if he told them that he had lost the money playing? Would they ever trust him now?

When he came in sight of his house all the family were on the steps waiting for him.

"Timmy," they cried, "where have you been? Why are you so late? Where is the sewing box? You found there was none, didn't you?"

Timothy's mother ran down the steps to him. "Why are you so late, dear?" she asked. "We were worried."

Timothy swallowed. It was hard to tell. "I had to go all the way to Harold's house," he began, and bit by bit, hard as it was, Timmy told his story: how he had played with Harold, lost the money, found Harold's and taken it to his home.

"I wanted to use it, Mother, to buy you a birthday present," he said.

"I know," his mother answered, putting her arm around him, "but you have given me the best birthday present I could have—an honest son. It was honest of you to take Harold's money to him at once. It was honest and truthful for you to tell us how you lost the silver piece. We know now that when Timothy speaks, he is speaking the truth."

102

"But Mother," one of the brothers spoke, "do you really believe there is such a thing as a musical sewing box?"

"If Timmy says so, I do," she said, just as footsteps were heard.

Harold came running up the road, holding something in his hand. Timothy ran to open the gate for him, and Harold stopped, panting for breath.

"Your sewing box," he said. "I was hunting for my silver piece and found yours. I knew it was to buy the sewing box for your mother's birthday, so I bought it for you and ran all the way to have it here on time. If you open the cover you will hear the tune."

"*Thank* you, Harold!" was all Timothy could say before he ran with the box to his mother, while the brothers and sisters stood amazed to hear the music box play. At last they had to believe their little brother.

From that time on there was a change in Timothy's family, for now it was Timothy who was given the important errands to do. "He is sure to bring back a true account," the others said. And Timmy it was who was asked now, when anything special occurred, "Just how did that happen, Timmy?"

So it came to be the fashion in that family, and in all the neighborhood, to say, "If Timmy says it, it is true. You can count on him as you can count on the sun rising and setting each day."

Pause after the Story

Song: "Maker of the Planets" (page 236).

Music for Leaving
(It was at this time that Virginia set to music the Bible verse used in this service and found on page 231.)

"WINTER DAY, FROSTY DAY"

It has been snowing all night. Children come into their rooms looking like small lively snowmen. Caps, coats, hair and eyelashes are frosted, but voices are gay, telling of stars that have fallen on sleeves, but which have melted, alas, too quickly to capture; or sharing enjoyment of the transformed landscape, and of the opportunities for fun in the snow.

Such is the excitement in the various classes over the snow that the supervisor changes her plan for the service of worship. Teachers have rifled the picture file for photographs of snowflakes, and their memories for the rules for folding paper to cut out six-pointed stars.

Snowflakes in their combination of uniformity and beauty of design not only make an interesting study, but are an inspiration to worship. The exquisite beauty of the individual crystals, the repetition of the six-sided or six-pointed pattern, the fact that no two crystals have ever been found alike, make a deep impression on the children.

The leader who wishes to be prepared for snowy Sunday mornings will find background material for the story of Wilson Bentley, the first man ever to make the photographing of snowflakes a lifework, in the book on *Snowflakes* found in public libraries and natural history museums. A study of the atmospheric conditions for the different formations of the flakes, shared with the children, must add to their growing consciousness of an orderly universe.

Slides made from Mr. Bentley's photographs are available to schools and church schools for a nominal rental fee from the school service department of such museums as the American Museum of Natural History in New York.

The story of Wilson Bentley's research is also found in *Children's Worship in the Church School* where he is erroneously called Hugh.

Two services of Worship used on snowy mornings follow:

I

Leader (after the usual Calls to Worship): I wish we had a good winter song. Let's name over what we like about the snow, perhaps we can make one.

Children: It's so quiet and still.

We have fun sliding.

We make hills of snow, and then pour water on them, and it changes to ice, and makes it slippery for our sleds.

We can skate in winter.

Yes, and go skiing, too.

When it snows I like to go out and feel it, it's so light, like feathers.

The snow makes pretty scenes.

The seeds don't die all winter long. I think it's wonderful that they don't die all the winter months.

It sparkles like diamonds.

When I came to church school it was on all the bushes and the wires, and pulled them down.

Leader: This is what someone long ago said about winter. It is in the Bible, and is speaking of God: "He giveth snow like wool . . . He casteth forth his ice like morsels" (A.S.V.).

And someone else, long ago, in the Bible, asked: "Hast thou entered the treasuries of the snow?" (A.S.V.).

I wonder what he was thinking of when he said "treasuries." A treasury is usually where money and precious jewels are kept.

Another verse, like a prayer is one we could sing now.

Song: Open our eyes that we may behold
      wondrous things out of thy law;
   Open our eyes that we may behold
      wondrous things out of thy law!

Leader: We have often spoken about God's laws. Sometimes we call them the laws or ways of nature, like the rules for seeds, and stars; like the laws Dr. Carver studied, the laws for peanuts, and sweet potatoes, and their different parts combining to make other products. The first grade has made a tune to some words about the law which a raindrop follows when it drops, and runs toward the sea, and then is dashed up in spray, to be drawn up in the air again.

First-grade Song (words by Lucy Sprague Mitchell):

Sea, spray, clouds, rain: Snow and riv - er and sea a - gain.

Dorothy Ann's Poem (made the year before, when she discovered another law):

> Snowflakes make stars:
> Once when I was going in our door
> A star fell on me.

Story: Wilson Bentley, The Snowflake Man

Closing Song:
> Hark to the sound
> Of chiming bells
> List to the song
> Their music tells
> "Praise ye, praise God!"

> Praise him for friends
> Who help us know
> Wonders of God
> The world may show.
> Praise God for friends!

II

"HAST THOU ENTERED THE TREASURIES OF THE SNOW?"

Stereopticon slides of frost patterns, snowflakes and snow scenes had been borrowed from the museum for this service.

Prayer (after quiet music for entering, and a Call to Worship sung): Maker of our world of wonders, we have come again to this quiet place to think about you and the world you have made. Whether it is winter or summer, if we search we find wonders on every hand, surprises in the commonest things about us; and beauty in unexpected places. Open our eyes, Lord, that we may behold again wondrous things out of thy law.

Song: "Heigh-ho for Snow!" (made from earlier contributions, put together by supervisor and music supervisor, who had in a third-grade music period helped the children to create a tune for it. Music and words on page 238).

Bible Verse: Hast thou entered the treasuries of the snow?

Conversation about what writer could have been thinking of.

Explanation about the slides to be shown, and the poems which would accompany them, like music.

Slide (colored, of snow scene showing twigs thickly covered).

Poem "Winter Beauties" by Florence Taylor:

> The winter air is crisp and cold,
>   The snow lies deep.
> Beneath their frosty coverlet
>   The flowers sleep.
>
> And on each smallest bit of twig,
>   Shining and bright,
> Hang rainbow-tinted icicles
>   That catch the light.
>
> The colors of the summer flowers
>   Still shine and glow,
> Whenever sunlight sparkles on
>   The brilliant snow.

Slide (of farm house and farm implements almost buried in snow).

107

Poem "Great White World" by Annette Wynne:

> Great white world beyond the window sill,
> White fence, white tree, white cart, white hill,
> You lie outside all calm and still
> As if the ground were never green
> And buttercups were never seen,
> And red and blue things in the grass
> For all the children that may pass,
> And twitterings and buzzings, too,
> That make us listen passing through;
> But now a hush is in the air—
> A blanket's spread out everywhere
> And all the world is white and still,
> White fence, white tree, white cart, white hill.

Slide: Frost on window pane.

Poem "Frost" by Hannah Flagg Gould:

> He went to the windows of those who slept
> And over each pane like a fairy crept.
> Wherever he breathed, wherever he stept,
> By the light of the moon was seen
> Most beautiful things. There were flowers and trees,
> There were bevies of birds, and swarms of bees,
> There were cities, thrones, temples, and towers, and these
> All pictured in silver sheen.

Snowflake Crystal Slides. An introduction reminded children to notice the number of *points* or *sides* each flake had—depending on how much had melted. (The simpler, six-sided flakes, and sometimes three-sided, are formed in colder air and not melted down into star-shapes, but all star shapes are six-pointed.)

Poem "Snow" by William Cullen Bryant:

> Here delicate snow-stars, out of the cloud
> Come floating down in airy play,

Like spangles dropped from the glistening crowd
That whiten by night the Milky Way.

Song Response (sung, as in a litany, after each subsequent
snowflake slide shown, to avoid mounting oh's and ah's):

We can but watch and wonder.

Closing Song: Praise God for friends
Who help us know
Wonders of God
The world may show.

Music for Leaving: "Maker of the Planets."

NEW LIFE IN SPRING

It is spring. The Polyphemus cocoon which has been
cherished all winter long is handled eagerly but ever so
carefully, for whatever is inside is stirring! Something that
looked dead has life.

Budding branches and tadpoles are brought into class-
rooms. Everywhere spring is in the air and children are
constantly discovering evidences of new life.

In the department where these services developed, experiences with nature include many experiences with people. For persons are a part of the world of nature, subject
to laws of life, growth and change as surely as are plants
and animals. Through contacts with social agencies in the
community, groups of boys and girls have become conscious of laws of cause and effect in other realms than
what we usually call "nature": laws affecting health, happiness, and consequently usefulness of people; laws having
to do with growth of mind and spirit.

Twice second- and third-grade classes in the church
school have been entertained by children in schools for the
blind, which led to stories of Louis Braille and of Samuel
Gridley Howe, founder of the Perkins Institute for the

Blind. Most thrilling of all was the story of little Helen Keller and the changes which came about through her teacher, Anne Sullivan.

These groups have also recently made a trip to a Settlement House in a down-town section, to play on the roof with the children cared for in clubs and classes in the Settlement, and heard the story of the need of and founding of such institutions.

Services like the following bring together the experiences and thought of several groups, and link themselves naturally to the Christian celebration of Palm Sunday and Easter.

A SERVICE FOR PALM SUNDAY

On the Easel: Picture of Palm Sunday.
Spring Music (as children gather).
A *Spring Song from the Bible:* Psalm 104:10, 13, 14, 15c, 16, 17, 18, 24, *or* Song of Solomon 2:11, 12.
Song Refrain (when above verses are used as a litany) on page 231 ("Oh, God, how wonderful").
Song: "Blue Sky, Soft and Clear."
Conversation about Spring
Song: "Praise Be to God There Comes" (page 235).
Reference to Cocoons and a Recent Experience

(Referring to the recent visit to the Lighthouse for the Blind, and the play given by the children there, the leader said that the cocoons made her think of the visit, for something she saw there made her think of cocoons. There was a little girl named Audrey who reminded her of a cocoon. Could the children here think why?

(Several remembered Audrey, and one volunteered, "Because she was so still." "That was exactly it," the leader said. "She seemed all wound up within herself, or all shut inside something, as if she couldn't come out. You remember that the teacher told us that Audrey had just begun coming to

110

the school. There was another little girl there named Theresa"—more recognizing nods—"who reminded me, not of a moth hidden away, and wound around with many wrappings, but of a moth which had come out of its cocoon."

("The way she flew around and jumped up and down," the children suggested at once, remembering the liveliness and freedom of eight-year-old Theresa, who had been attending the school since Nursery days.)

Picture of Palm Sunday and Talk:

Today we are celebrating in our churches a day called Palm Sunday. It is in memory of a day when Jesus rode into the city of Jerusalem, with a crowd of people who loved him and wanted to honor him. They even wanted to make him their king. They cut branches from the trees and waved them in the air and scattered them along the road, as they might for a royal person. And they sang "Hosanna, Hosanna!" (That has a prettier sound than our "Hooray!")

In that crowd I think there were people for whom Jesus had made the world seem as different as it must to blind children when they begin to lose their fear of moving about and know they can do for themselves what friends have had to do for them before. They, too, had been afraid of the world, afraid of people, afraid of falling, afraid of even trying out their own powers. When Jesus cured their fears they discovered they were able to do what they never thought they could.

There are stories of any number of persons who had been like little Audrey—like cocoons, all in tight bindings, thinking they would never be any happier because they were different from others. Nobody would ever like them, they probably thought: they'd never be of any use. Then Jesus came along. "I like you," his eyes seemed to say, and before they knew it he was making them believe new things about themselves. "Come," he would say, "God gave you powers you have not yet tried."

And when they tried, they found it was true! Some, who

111

believed they could not walk, walked. Some who had never thought much for themselves, began to think. Some who had never helped anyone began to have pleasant feelings of knowing they *could* help, and trying it. Some who had cheated their neighbors began to want to pay back all they had taken unfairly. Some who had always been afraid of what the soldiers or other important people in the land would say or do, took courage, and were surprised to find how much courage they had!

Jesus had discovered a rule or a law about life that is as truly a law as that snowflakes have six sides, or that spring follows winter. It was a law "his heart had learned from God." It told him that to change a person who is all bound up (like a cocoon) with fears and sickness and bad thinking, one must be a friend to that person and help him believe in the powers in him that he has never tried.

Music (played softly): "Tell Me the Stories of Jesus."

Singing of New Stanza for "Tell Me the Stories of Jesus" (made from suggestions of third-grade class dramatizing story of Zacchaeus, who wanted another verse to the song which would show how Jesus "changed" people whose sickness, fears or friendlessness kept them from happiness and usefulness):

> Tell how the sick and the suff'ring
> From fear or pain,
> Feeling the power of his healing,
> Grew strong again.
> Friend of the friendless,
> Lonely or sad,—
> Tell how he changed them
> And made them glad.

Prayer: God, from whom come all laws of life and growth and change, we thank you that we may study these laws and know how to work with you. We thank you for the stories of Jesus who had learned the rule of kindness and friendliness and love. May we keep this law in our hearts, that we too may know how to help those we know to be freer and happier. In the spirit of Jesus we pray. Amen.

Song (or music of): "Lord, I Want to Be Like Jesus in My Heart."

EASTER

This service provides for a continuation of the Palm Sunday talk, and for the showing of nature films from the museum. There are beautiful ones of slow motion, showing the opening of flowers from buds; others of the life cycle of moths, butterflies, dragon flies, etc. If the time-lapse photography of growing, blossoming and fading of field and woodland flowers is used, the process of taking the pictures in order to show every stage unfolding should be explained to the chidlren, or the speeding up of the natural processes may be confusing. Any films or slides borrowed from museums should be tried out before showing for possible elimination of an undesirable portion, such as that which shows how to catch, kill and mount butterflies.

The service begins with Easter music, songs and verses familiar to each class. The picture on the easel is the same as for Palm Sunday.

Talk

You remember that we were thinking last Sunday about the men and women and children in this picture and how some of them, waving branches, might be the very persons who had thought once that they would always be sick and helpless. Jesus showed them they had power within them that they had never used, and some found that if they believed they could, even though they had been lame, they could walk, and some who had been blind and helpless could be like other people. But they never would have tried, perhaps, if he had not shown them that he cared.

We can imagine crowds listening to Jesus as he gave his

113

rules for living: *Love one another; Do good to them that hate you; Do to others what you would like others to do to you; Love your enemies.*

That day when people greeted him and went before him, waving branches, they called him king. They really wanted him for a king. And all the rulers said, "This will never do! If he should ever have power over us, we should have to stop doing what we do to make money and to make everybody do as we say. We are not going to have him telling us how to run our business. No, let us kill him, and get rid of him."

So they killed him. They said, "Now he is dead, we are rid of him. He and his teaching will trouble us no more!" But they were not rid of him.

At first his friends were very sad. They had hoped for great things. If Jesus *had* been made a king, they knew it would have been happier for them. It would be wonderful to be a friend of a king. But now he was dead, they didn't see any use in anything any more. They didn't feel like working or doing anything worth while.

Then something happened. It was as if that power that was in Jesus, that spirit that made him what he was, had suddenly become alive again. It was so real and so near that one after another said they had *seen* Jesus! Some said he had come to them and talked to them. Whatever happened, they began to be of use again. Some discovered, to their joy, that they had the same kind of power to help people that Jesus had. And the rulers, instead of getting rid of one man and his ideas, found that others were doing the same works that Jesus had done. It was just as if Jesus had risen from the dead, and was working many times as hard in the very ways that had made the rulers angry.

There were Peter and John, who went one day to the temple and found a lame beggar by the door. They spoke to him as Jesus would have spoken, they put out their hands and helped him to stand up. They gave him what Jesus would have given him—strength to walk and go about his work. When the rulers heard about it and that Peter and

John were preaching and teaching the same rules that Jesus had taught, they put them both in jail. But the next day they had escaped from jail, and went right on teaching in public places.

There was a man named Stephen who preached and taught. The rulers said they would kill him, and they did, but there was another man named Paul standing by, and before long Paul was preaching, too, and starting churches everywhere. He sailed away to other lands, and preached and taught and wrote letters to help everyone know more about Jesus. We read those letters in our Bibles today.

Jesus was living more than ever before! His spirit was going on and on, making people share what they knew, helping to heal the sick, to teach love and friendliness in cities, in lonely mountain places, in foreign lands. The life, the spirit that was in Jesus, could never die. Today there are thousands and thousands of teachers and ministers and doctors and missionaries and helpers in children's homes, hospitals, schools for the deaf and blind, settlements and neighborhood houses, all with the spirit of Jesus, having learned the law he knew, the law of friendliness.

Prayer: O God, whose spirit was in Jesus, we thank thee that Jesus lived and that his spirit never died.

We thank thee that it is more alive today than when he lived here on earth, and that we ourselves have seen it working in children's homes and church centers and schools, to bring health and friendship and happiness and love to boys and girls and older people. May part of that spirit be in us, and may we help to spread it. Amen.

Song: "Lord, I Want to Be Like Jesus in My Heart."

Movie or Slides of some of nature's changes.

Song (played as children leave): "Praise Be to God There Comes."

VI

"Circles"

The services in this series are designed to increase the children's observation and appreciation of the "riches" about them and of the cyclic order of some of Nature's changes; to help them discover similar laws at work in their own relationships and lives.

THE GIFT OF SEEING EYES

After the usual quieting music, a call to worship and suitable song, Psalm 119:18 is read, introduced by the comment that it was used as a prayer long ago by people who were constantly making new discoveries about God's laws.

Song: "Open Our Eyes That We May Behold" (page 231).

Story or Talk (suited to the local situation), e.g.:

Have you ever been to a museum? Do you remember your first visit, and what were the most interesting things you saw? . . .

Two girls and a boy stood in the first room of a big museum. The boy had been there before, but for the girls, it was their first visit. Tom, the boy, was having a good time. "I'll show you all my favorite exhibits," he said, and laughed as the eyes of the girls grew bigger and bigger with wonder. There were butterflies and birds and shells and seaweed. "Why, I never knew there were so many kinds," Alice would exclaim, and Mary, "And I never knew they could be so pretty!"

"Oh, look," Alice would say, "did you notice this?" and at the same time Mary would call, "Oh, come over here and look in this case! Why hadn't I ever seen this before?"

For there before them, in case after case, in room after room, were treasures from woods and fields and earth and skies and oceans. Tom felt as if he owned that museum and was so pleased to be sharing its wonders with friends. It was his museum in two ways: first, just as it belonged to the girls, for it was a city museum, built for everybody. But then it was his in a special way, too, for he had made it his. Each time he visited it he made new exciting discoveries though the treasures were there always for those with eyes to see.

Now the children wondered together at curious and beautiful things they saw. There was the stump of a giant redwood tree, for instance, with hundreds and hundreds of circular markings, beginning with quite small rings in the center, and larger and larger ones as they traveled toward the outside bark. The sign on the stump said that each ring meant a year of growth. Spaces between rings were very narrow sometimes, sometimes broader. That meant, the sign said, that in the dry years the tree did not grow very much, so the spaces were small. The years when there was plenty of rain the tree grew faster and the spaces were bigger. My, the children thought, how did anyone ever figure that out? But here it was, all worked out for them so they could tell that that tree, when it was cut down, was eighteen hundred years old! Wasn't it wonderful, they thought, that there were ways to tell the age of trees, and in just what years they grew fastest!

In what looked like a great big tank in another room there were strange fish of lovely colors and pretty shapes. The signs told just what kind of fish they were, and where they lived, and what water plants grew near; what the fish ate, and how they protected themselves. It was the same in the rooms with animals, and the rooms with birds. How many,

117

many interesting things to find out about the world, different laws for each living thing—but laws which people could study and find were always the same.

Tom and the girls went away from the museum with a feeling of gladness for having found something new, to be theirs forever.

Story (Outline): The Purse of Gold and the Seeing Eye[1]

This is a fairy tale of two brothers, one who shared his food with the fairies, and they loved him. Wishing to give him a gift, they gave him the precious one of seeing eyes. As he went back home from the fairy ring in the woods, he kept seeing interesting and beautiful sights he'd never noticed before. The woods seemed his, now, in a new way. He could hardly wait to share his new gift with his brother, and with his friends.

His brother, on hearing that the fairies had presented a gift in return for food left out at night for them, told the boy he was a fool not to have asked for something really valuable. What good were seeing eyes? Why hadn't his brother asked for a purse of gold?

He would show his brother that he himself would do better. He began leaving some of his supper out for the fairies, not because he wanted to share it, but because he wanted to be rewarded. After six nights he visited the fairy ring and demanded a reward. He had left food out six nights now, and deserved a gift from the fairies, he declared. When the little man in the peaked hat, who had talked with his brother, asked him what he wanted, the greedy brother said, "A purse of gold."

The little man said fairies didn't put much store by purses of gold, but it might be arranged. Elated, and suddenly given as much gold as he could ever wish for, the greedy brother became discontented with the hut in the woods, bought a house in town, would not have anything to do with

[1] Originally from *The Bluebird's Garden* by Patten Beard, now out of print. To be found in *The Children's Story Garden* by Anna Pettit Broomell (Lippincott).

neighbors for fear they might want something from him, but made enemies right and left. He won more and more possessions, but fewer and fewer friends, while the brother whom the fairies loved, who was constantly sharing his discoveries in field and wood, was blessed with more and more friends, and was happy to the day of his death.

Poem:

> Open mine eyes that I may behold
> Treasures more precious than silver or gold:
> Riches forever to have and to hold!

Hymn, second stanza of "For the Beauty of the Earth":

> For the wonder of each hour
>   Of the day and of the night,
> Hill and vale and tree and flower,
>   Sun and moon and stars of night,
> Lord of all, to thee we raise,
> This our hymn of grateful praise.

Things That Belong to Us All

The Call to Worship and a praise song are followed by a period of meditation, in which the thinking is directed toward "things that belong to us all" which we do not ordinarily notice.

Story (of incident in the life of Alice Freeman Palmer, recorded by George Herbert Palmer in his biography of his wife):

At one time Mrs. Palmer worked in a settlement in one of Boston's poorer districts and often met groups of children for stories, etc. One day, and to her surprise, a child asked, "Tell us how to be happy."

Mrs. Palmer, reflecting on the drab and burdened life of these "little mothers," hardly knew how to answer, but then told them about a bit of "magic" which, if practiced every day, would bring happiness. A day must not be skipped, however, she made it clear, or the magic would not work. One must find something pretty every day, and memorize some verse or bit of poetry each day, and do something helpful for someone every single day.

As she left them, and thought about her recipe for happiness, she was not too pleased with it. What could these children, surrounded by ugliness, find of beauty? As for being helpful, their lives were made up of "doing for others."

A few days later, as she was walking across the Common, she felt a tug at her sleeve and looked down into a child's grimy face turned up to hers with eagerness. It was a shabby little girl who was saying proudly, "I done it!" "Did what?" Mrs. Palmer asked. "What you said," the child replied. "It was awful hard, sometimes, but I found something pretty every day. One day I couldn't go out, and I thought sure I'd never see anything pretty, and then I looked, and the sun was shining on the baby's hair, and it was all gold. And another day it rained all day, and I couldn't see much from the window. Then I saw some sparrows getting a drink from the eaves trough, and they had black neck-ties on! So I didn't skip a day!"

Leader: Let's close our eyes while Miss H—— plays some music, and in the quiet let us try to see in our imaginations other sights which people even in ugly parts of our city, such as we saw the other day, can see and find beautiful.

Responses. (It is often awe-inspiring to listen to children's ideas of beauty as reflected in an experience of this kind. In one service children who had recently visited a section in their city comparable to Mrs. Palmer's settlement neighborhood gave all these flashes of beauty:)

The sun on bright red fire engines as they go by.

The blue sky with little white clouds.

The bright searchlights over the sky at night.

The sun on silver planes going through the sky.

The round moon and shining stars.

The rainbow colors in a mud puddle.

The splash of little drops splitting and catching the light as the rain falls.

The sun on long icicles hanging from the walls.

The trees: red leaves in the autumn, the snow covering the branches in winter, the buds coming out in the spring.

Leader: And these are "things that belong to us all." We can make their beauty ours forever—and always have riches to share!

> Open mine eyes that I may behold
> Treasures more precious than silver or gold,
> Riches forever to have and to hold.

Song: "For the Beauty of the Earth."

"The Earth Is Full of Thy Riches"

To Have on the Table: Branches with opening buds.
Verses to Use: "O God, how manifold are thy works. . . . The earth is full of thy riches."
Recall of last Sunday's story and discussion.
A Spring Song, or "For the Beauty of the Earth."

Poem (made from children's contributions last week, or the following, read slowly, pauses after each line):

"God Giveth Us Richly All Things To Enjoy"

"Open mine eyes that I may behold"—
Wealth that is mine, unimagined, untold:

In fields and in woods, by the shore, in the air,
A fortune to find—a fortune to share!

Gold in the sunset, silver in rain;
Priceless designs in the frost on my pane;

121

Jewels that glitter, like diamonds, in snow;
Color and patterns wherever I go:

Spirals and curves of most delicate grace,
Cob-webby threads making filmiest lace;

Stories in rocks, and songs in the breeze,
Magic in gray cocoons hanging from trees;

Pictures in clouds as they roll gently by,
Unwritten poems in a star-lit sky,

O God of the wind, and the sky and the sea,
I thank thee for giving such riches to me!

Prayer (or Suggestions for Directed Meditation):

God, we come here this morning from a world outside that speaks of you on every hand, but we may have been too busy thinking of other things, or hurrying too fast to notice your work.

It is quiet here now. We have time to remember that "the earth is full of thy riches," and to name some over in our minds. (Pause.) We have time to remember how a child in an ugly part of a city could still find something beautiful. We have time to think of what is happening outside these days; they are happenings that would go right on, whether we were here or not, whether there were people living here or not. For people have nothing to do with these happenings. They are "the Lord's doing," "we can but watch and wonder." May we remember some of these happenings now . . .

Prayer Song: "Open Our Eyes," etc.

Conversation about Branches and Leaf Buds. (An appreciation of one of nature's cycles stimulated by observation of twigs with open leaf buds: Facts brought out about how the sap —mineral water mixed and enriched by the decayed vegetable matter in the soil—starts its upward flow in the spring;

how, when it reaches the little leaf buds, they begin to open. Pale at first, as the chlorophyll in the leaf gathers and begins its work of manufacturing food which is carried to all parts of the tree throughout the summer. Summer ended, the leaf's work is over, and chlorophyll is withdrawn. Leaf changes color, finally loosening hold on the branch as a new leaf bud forms and pushes it off. The old leaf drops to the ground and becomes part of the very soil that feeds the tree, while the new leaf, tightly wrapped and encased in a waterproof coat, is all ready for the impetus to unfold and grow which the spring flow of sap will give again.)

Other Cycles. The children will think of other "circles" seemingly having no beginning and no end; the rain cycle, seeds and flowers, caterpillar and butterfly, day and night, seasons, etc.

Poem: "Over and Over Again" (leaf stanza), or entire poem (page 194).

Cycle Rhythm (see Chapter VIII).

Song: "The Sun Is Gone Down," "Glad That I live am I," or "Praise Be to God There Comes."

"While The Earth Remaineth"

Music to Play: Chopin's "Raindrop Prelude."

A Call to Worship:
>Sing to him, make music to him,
>go over all the wonders he has done.
>
>(Moffatt)

Two Other Verses from the Bible:
>For lo, the winter is past;
>The rain is over and gone;
>The flowers appear on the earth;
>The time of the singing of birds is come.

While the earth remaineth, seedtime and harvest, and cold and heat, and summer and winter and day and night shall not cease.

A Song: One of the "Cycle" songs mentioned above, or "For the Beauty of the Earth," or "Round and Round," (page 240), read slowly to the music or sung by a teacher, or learned before this service.

Story (a "Cycle" story): "The Road That Wanted to Be Beautiful" by Carolyn Sherwin Bailey, or "The Mustard Seed" as told in *The Story-Teller in Religious Education,* or "Buried Sunshine," a story made by the leader of sun warming and helping to grow, millions of years ago, great forests of trees and ferns; of their falling in swamps and lying there for ages; earthquakes which folded them far below the surface of the earth; water and pressure changing them into something other than wood; men today digging in the earth to discover layers and layers of coal—the ancient trees—to give out again the light and heat once absorbed from the sun.

A Prayer: God, Giver of all life, we thank you that for every sleeping thing there is a waking-up time; that for every living thing there is a "living again" time. We thank you that we may say of anyone, and that anyone may say of us, "You are not yet all that you are going to be." Amen.

Can People Make Circles?

The leader of one group, to introduce the story, "The Song that Traveled," asked if people could start circles. She told of going down the street one day, facing the sun, and not realizing that her face was screwed into a squint. A stranger passed, and smiled. The leader, thinking what a pleasant person this was to smile at a perfect stranger, smiled back, but found that her mouth was already stretched to capacity in a wide grin—or squint. Then she understood why the stranger had smiled: she had mistaken the squint for a smile, which made her want to return the friendliness, which made the leader try to smile back again! The children talked about scowling, and of how "somebody else might think you were cross, and act cross, too, which would make you crosser."

One said you started a circle when you wrote a letter— the other person wrote back to you, and you wrote again, etc.

The illustrations suggested a law of cause and effect which, like those laws observed in nature's cycles, was one of God's laws. If people understood them better they might realize what kind of action might bring certain results, and get along better with one another. Was the singer in the Bible long ago thinking of something like this when they prayed: "Teach me thy way, O Lord. . . . Give me understanding and I shall keep thy law?"

Maud Lindsay's classic story from her book, *The Story-Teller*, was an example of a "circle" in the lives of persons. "The Song That Travelled" gives the travels of a song originated by a happy king in his palace on a sunny spring day. Caught in turn by a plowboy in the field adjoining the palace grounds, by a goosegirl on the next farm, by the peddler from whom the goosegirl buys a ribbon for her hair, by a soldier home from the wars, and by a sailor just going to sea, the song returns after a year and a day by way of a minstrel on the sailor's ship to the king himself at his Mayday festival.

Prayer: "Teach me thy way, O God!" As we see the working of thy laws in the world of nature, we see it too among people. May we notice what our words and our acts bring back to us, to go forth again perhaps with greater force. May the ways we choose to act be ways we should like to have practiced toward us. May we remember always the rule Jesus gave.

Music of "As Ye Would" (page 232).

The laws governing the interrelationship among people are as subject to interference as are the laws of interaction between forces of nature.

Nature is always seeking perfection, but rarely attains it. Interference of some sort usually prevents the forming of a perfect specimen. Storm winds or lightning may work against the symmetry of a tree; insects may stop the normal growth of plants; crowding from without or within may keep atoms or molecules from forming a perfect crystal. (This last the children had observed in their experiments with salt and sugar crystals, and with snowflakes.)

In all the world of nature only human beings have been given the power of choosing whether they will work with the laws for growth and perfection, or against them. Only to persons, out of all life, is it given to compare experiences and results; to see how effect follows cause, and how the ignoring of the laws for individual growth and successful co-operative living sets in motion the laws for preventing progress, and even destruction of life itself.

Two stories are outlined here to suggest our own responsibility in starting or preventing a "circle" of a destructive kind.

The first is a story of Heinrich, a refugee who had worn the same suit of clothes since he escaped from Germany two years before.

In his American school the boys and girls persecuted Heinrich unmercifully. They made fun of his clothes; they mocked his intonations and pronunciation; they called him a Nazi. He was left out of games on the playground and ignored except as he was the victim of bullies who thought it smart to fight him and put gum in his hair. He was made to understand by them that this was all because of Hitler, as if Heinrich were somehow to blame.

"Don't you just hate Hitler?" Heinrich said bitterly to his mother.

"No, I don't hate Hitler," his mother replied after a moment. "I don't hate Hitler, but I hate the things he does. I hate to see people hurt, because of what it does to them inside. There is a story that *he* was hurt when he was young, and he wanted to get even. I suppose he started a boy like you, and then when he was hurt by someone began to have angry feelings and wanted to hurt other people. Of course," she said, "*you can decide*, because you are hurt now, to grow up and try to get even with him, and hurt many other people while you are doing it. Everybody has to decide for himself how he will act."

Shortly after that when the children on the playground were particularly mean to Heinrich and he fought them off, and they retaliated with stones which broke a window, he was ready to report at once to the teacher that he knew which child threw the stone. His feelings were still sore; then he remembered another whose hurt made him want to "get even," and rather than be like Hitler, remembering that it was for him to decide, he took the blame of the stone-throwing, laying it to the fight. The other children, impressed with his generosity in not telling on them, confessed that they started the whole thing by being mean to him, and at last saw how unfair they had been, told him they were ashamed, and took him into their games, even making him captain. He had broken a circle—an evil one—and started a good one.

The other story is of a time when Jesus and his disciples were walking through a village in Samaria (Luke 9:51-55).

The party was walking to Jerusalem, the capital city of the Jews. Jesus had sent messengers on ahead to find food and a place for them to stop and rest.

They hastened back to tell Jesus what had happened.

127

They were furious. The people in the village had made it quite plain that they wanted none of them, neither Jesus nor his friends, nor anyone on his way to Jerusalem. It all went back to an old, old quarrel between the Jews and Samaritans long before these people or their grandfathers were born. But the hard feelings on both sides continued, so that now, after all these years, anyone known to be traveling toward the great city of the Jews was refused any kind of hospitality.

"What shall we do to them?" they angrily asked Jesus.

"Let's pray for a fire to burn up the whole town!" they said, making believe they were ready to start the fire themselves.

But Jesus, the story says, "rebuked" them, and they went to another village.

"Rebuke" means to reprove sharply. It sounds as if Jesus saw another "circle" starting, and broke it off short. He had rules for living and getting along with others which would keep people from hurting one another.

Some of Jesus' Rules:
>Love your enemies.
>Do good to them that hate you.
>Do to others what you would have them do to you.

A Song to Sing: "As Ye Would . . ."

"You Are More than the Earth"

Quiet Music: "Round and Round" (Dvořák's *Largo*) and "Maker of the Planets."

Call to Worship (sung):
>Quiet our minds and our spirits
>Until new thoughts come,
>We will go over in our minds
>The wonders you have done:
>Thank you, God.

Picture: Taylor's "When I Consider Thy Heavens."

Leader: Once long ago a man stood, like this man in the picture, looking up into the night. He felt small beside the
great world that God had created. He talked with God about
it. He said something like this: "God, when I consider your
heavens, the moon and the stars and the planets, what is
man, that you should think of him?"

Many people have had this question. Some have found
answers. Perhaps you will think of one. In a little while I'll
read a poem which gives one answer. Let's close our eyes
and think about this great big universe we're born into.

Meditation: First I'll name what I think of, and then you name
what you think of that goes with it.

I think of the green earth spread so far on every side that
no one can see it all. What do you see growing, in your
imaginations? (Children name trees, flowers, etc.)

Then I think of the sea. I see waves dashing high, and
then rolling back. What makes them do that? (Children
probably speak of tides.)

Now I am thinking of the wind that blows, and what it
brings with it. (Children may mention clouds, rain, etc.)

Now I am thinking of the skies, and what I see there in
the daytime and at night. (Children name what comes to
their minds.)

Some of these things suggest circles to me, but they are
circles that no person could start or stop. (When children
name some of nature's cycles, suggest singing the "Cycle"
song.)

Song: "Round and Round" (first stanza, or second [see page
240] on chart, or previously learned, or sung by teacher to
Largo music).

Meditation (continued): For everything we have named there
are laws: for all growing things, for tides in the ocean; for
the stars and planets in the skies, for the seasons—even for
persons who watch it all, and think about it. We are like
every other thing which has been created, in one way—we

129

all have to follow laws if we grow as we are meant to grow. But in another way we are different. Do you know what way that is? . . .

This is the poem I said I would read:

Poem: "The Great World" by William Brighty Rand:

> Great, wide, beautiful, wonderful world,
> With the wonderful water round you curled,
> And the wonderful grass upon your breast,
> World, you are beautifully dressed!
>
> . . .
>
> Ah, you are so great, and I am so small,
> I tremble to think of you, world, at all;
> And yet, when I said my prayers today,
> A whisper inside me seemed to say,
> "You are more than the Earth, though only a dot;
> You can love, and think, and the Earth cannot."

Leader: Only *persons* have been given the power to choose what sort of circles they want to start and which they want to break. Let's think of some which people have started. . . . Which were good, and which were bad? . . .

Sometimes the circles started accidentally. (Children may recall incident of the squint that started a succession of smiles, and the story, "The Song That Travelled.")

Accidental or not, only persons can decide whether the circles shall be broken. (The story of Heinrich or of Jesus journeying through Samaria.)

Solomon's Prayer:

There is a story in the Bible of a prince named Solomon who, on his father's death, became king. As Solomon grew up in his father's court he saw how much depended on his decisions. A king could help or hurt so many people! He could start good things which would keep bringing about more good, or bad things which would bring about more evil. Such responsibility almost frightened him. He felt like a little child, not knowing which way to turn. He would have

130

been really frightened if he had not known that God, who made the laws of good and evil, would help him.

"Give me an understanding heart," he prayed, "that I may discern between good and evil."

Solomon must have started many good "circles," because the Bible tells of such wise choices he made that he was called the wisest man in the world.

"Give me an understanding heart," he had prayed, "that I may know how to choose between good and evil!"

Song: "Maker of the Planets."

VII

Christmas

The minister in his sermon on Family Sunday has told of a dog's footprint in a fresh cement floor, an imprint which would always be there as long as the floor itself lasted.

A third grade has picked up the analogy he expanded, and has been finding answers to "What were the thoughts and acts of Jesus which left an imprint?"

Another third grade is interested in people from other lands who have contributed their gifts to America. They have dipped into the life of Edward Bok, and liked the story of his Dutch grandfather who planted seeds on a bleak and barren island. The island had been used by pirates for criminal purposes, but the seeds transformed it into one of beauty and usefulness, and a sanctuary for birds.

The parable of the mustard seed has been told in two grades, in the first simply as a story of the miracle of growth, in connection with their interest in seeds; in the third in connection with the Bok seed story and as an introduction to Jesus' references to the kingdom of heaven. Several children in all grades, it has been learned, are repeating the Lord's Prayer as a nightly practice.

Fall and Thanksgiving projects have been completed.

The second grade made a miniature Succoth Booth for the Thanksgiving service and dramatized the desert wanderings. From now on the department is looking toward Christmas. All classes will be hearing stories of Jesus, not of his birth, but of his life among his fellow men, his understanding of people's troubles and his immediate desire to help them; his understanding of God: a reminder to the older children, an introduction to the younger of the spirit of the one whose birthday we celebrate.

All this is in the background of the services which follow.

I

Prayer (by leader, after Music and Call to Worship, and lighting of candles): God, we have lighted one of our Thanksgiving candles for Jesus, whose birthday we celebrate soon. As we think about him on these Sundays before Christmas, may we understand why his friends loved him and followed him and how they learned from him about you. May we learn more about you as we think of him, and hear of what he did and said. Amen.

Song: One stanza of "Tell Me the Stories of Jesus."

Story (Outline): About four boys whose names were like four of our boys: James and John, Andrew, and Simon, whose name was changed to Peter. Lived on lake, fathers fishermen. From earliest childhood had known lake better than anything else. Waded in it, watched storms on it; in fine weather looked into clear depths which sometimes showed only clear water and grasses, sometimes great shoals of fishes; played in it, swam in it, fished in it, learned to row boats in it, and to clean nets of weeds caught in it. Probably thought they would always live and work in and on that lake; maybe would make plans about when they were grown up, and had a fishing business. Maybe thought they might be famous some day for that fishing business, and would send fish all over the world, as some men farther down the lake, a place called Tarachaea, were famous for their pickling business.

But something happened. One night, when they were grown, and handled the boats by themselves, and were already good fishermen, fished all night, but caught no fish. Tired, disappointed, discouraged, were cleaning nets by shore, and didn't notice at first that there were more people than usual on beach. Kept coming, men finally noticed. Quite a crowd, all around one man they couldn't see at first —until he walked down to the water and to Simon and Andrew's boat. He asked them to row him away from the shore a bit. He could talk more easily now, and more people could see him.

Wondering who this man was, whom the people called Jesus, they began to listen to what he was saying. James and John listened, too, from their boat.

He was talking about God. The fishermen knew about God; they had always heard of him, first in their homes, then in the synagogue school when they were boys. They had heard how God helped Moses to lead their people out of slavery in Egypt, and been with them all through their history. All Jewish boys knew of God. Even after they were grown they heard about him each Sabbath in the synagogue. But they thought of God as far away, more in their history than with them now.

This teacher called God *Father*. That seemed strange. "But fathers have children whom they care for," someone said.

"He cares for you," Jesus said. "He is your Father, too, your Father in heaven." People looked up at sky. "That is a long way off," they were probably thinking, but Jesus saw them.

"Heaven is not in the sky!" he said, shaking head kindly. The fishermen listened. Where was it, then, they wondered. But Jesus was already answering: "Heaven is *in you*—when you do as God wishes. That is what makes heaven." Simon and Andrew and James and John didn't understand. They

134

wanted to ask some questions. This man spoke as if he might know answers.

"Isn't God a kind of king?" someone wanted to know. Jesus: "He has a kingdom, but not the kind you are thinking of. It is small, like a mustard seed, but because it is in people doing as God wishes it grows and grows—like the mustard seed."

People still had questions. They asked each other, "How can his kingdom come here? How can we know his wishes?" But Jesus had noticed that the fishermen's boats were empty. And yet the men were cleaning their nets as if they had finished. He spoke to them. "Row out to deeper water," he told them, "and let down your nets."

Simon and Andrew didn't understand about the kingdom of heaven, but they thought they knew their lake. The fish were simply not biting that morning. Simon explained, "Master, we've been out all night and caught no fish—but—" it must have been something in Jesus' face that encouraged him, for he added, "—but if you say so, I'll let down the nets." Perhaps Jesus had looked out into the clear deep water and seen fish after all.

They let down the nets. Crowds and crowds of fishes swam into them—so many the four fishermen could hardly pull them in. The mass of fishes nearly broke the nets. It nearly sank the boats.

This teacher Jesus was wonderful, the men thought. He even knew their lake. What a friend to have! They wished he would stay with them by the lake.

Instead Jesus surprised them again. "Come with me," he said. He had important work to do, and they could help him, and he would teach them as they went about.

It must have been hard for those fishermen to decide whether or not to leave their fishing to join Jesus. It was almost as if your father were asked to leave his business, law, writing, or selling, and go up and down the country with a strange preacher. They would have no home. Where should they sleep? Where would he take them? How could

they help him, anyway? They had so much to learn themselves—they did not even understand about the "kingdom
of heaven" which he said was in them and could be right
here and now if—if—*what was it* that he had told them?
They must understand what he meant. They must learn
what this man had to teach them. And so they decided.
"They left all and followed him."

Quiet, after story, ending with musical phrase.

Leader: There is more to the story. We shall have the next
part next Sunday. Now I am going to make a prayer. It is
something like a part of the prayer that some of you know,
which Jesus taught.

Prayer: Our Father who art wherever thy wishes are done, may
thy kingdom come here, may thy wishes be done here. Amen.

II

How the Four Fishermen Learned

Quiet Music: "Tell Me the Stories of Jesus"; "Silent Night";
"Come Softly"; "I Heard the Bells on Christmas Day";
"Chimes."

Poem: "Christmas Time" by Nancy Byrd Turner:

> Christmas time is here again,
>   Christmas bells are ringing!
> Everywhere the wintry air
>   Is full of carol singing.
> By the fireside at home,
>   Down the lane and street,
> In the churches near and far,
>   We hear their music sweet.

Song: "O Come, All Ye Faithful."

Quiet Thinking and sharing of "Pictures" which come to mind
when the word "Christmas" is mentioned.

136

Prayer (made from these responses): God, our Father, we love to think of Christmas. It is full of (happy times), (gay shop windows), (lighted trees), (bells), (presents), (Christmas stories), etc. We thank you for the love in our hearts that makes us want to give presents to one another.

As we think today about Jesus whose birthday we celebrate soon, may we understand better why it is that people love to sing songs about the night he was born. Amen.

Song: "Silent Night."

Talk: e.g., We shouldn't have these Christmas songs we love if, when the baby we have sung about had not grown to be a man that left a deep *imprint* on the lives of people who watched and listened to him.

(Recall of four boys who became fishermen, how they first met Jesus, how curious they were to learn what Jesus had to teach them.) As they went about with him they listened ever so hard when he talked. They heard him say they must treat other people as they wanted to be treated themselves; that they must care about people, even those who had hurt them —care what happened to them. They must pray to God so he would know they wanted to do as he wished. They might say, "Our Father who art in heaven, may thy kingdom come here, may thy wishes be done here." They heard him say the kingdom of heaven was in them, and could grow and spread like a mustard seed.

Although they heard Jesus say these things, they did not always understand his words or even his stories. *But they could understand what he did.*

Let's follow them in imagination, and see if we can understand how they were learning.

They were probably proud to be asked to join Jesus. They might even have thought because of it they were a little better than others. I imagine them going with Jesus to the city. They had not learned to care about everyone then. There were many people in the city they didn't like. Men who collected tolls, for instance. (Explanation and compari-

137

son with tolls on bridges and entrances to the city by park-
ways. A regular charge, for "upkeep," but toll collectors in
that city could charge anything they liked and keep what
was left over. For that reason they were hated, for most of
them charged unfairly; thought of as "bad.")

Jesus came to gate of the city. Passed by Matthew. In
imagination I can see Simon-Peter and Andrew and James
and John looking down on Matthew, toll collector. Proud to
be seen with Jesus, maybe would have nothing at all to do
with a person like Matthew. Imagine their surprise when
they heard Jesus say—as if he *liked* Matthew—"Will you
come and help me? I have important work to do." That was
the same invitation that Jesus had given them! I imagine
them thinking, "There must be some good in him whom we
thought bad."

Another time they are sitting with Jesus on the porch of
the temple. (Description of the chests into which people
dropped their money. Twelve of them held gifts obligatory;
one of them, free-will offerings. When people put money in
that, it was because they wanted to. It was a way to share
what one had, because one was thankful.)

I imagine the thoughts of the fishermen as the rich men
put in their gifts, making much of the act. "Ah, here's an
important person," I imagine them saying. "Listen to the
sound of that coin dropping in. It's a big one." (They probably admired those with big gifts.) A poor woman comes.
Obviously she hasn't much to put in. Perhaps Andrew and
Peter and James and John don't even notice her—they have
probably turned heads aside to watch for next rich man. The
poor woman's coin makes the faintest tinkle. They hardly
hear it. If they do, they may think, "That's not much account!" But they hear Jesus, whose surprising words make
them suddenly turn around. (We hope the woman heard,
too, for maybe she thought, like them, that her gift wasn't
important.) "Look!" we can almost hear Jesus say. "Did you
see that poor woman? Did you see her put the coin in the
chest? She has given more than all the rest!"

138

The fishermen don't understand. Her coin was the smallest of all. But Jesus is explaining in words that make them see what really makes a gift big or little. "They had plenty left," he says; "she put in all she had." Jesus is teaching them what is important to God.

He heals a sick man on the Sabbath day. That is against the law in their books, and the rulers are angry. But Jesus says the good of people is more important than laws written in books.

He talks to people who are lonely, or afraid, or discouraged and think they're no good and never can do anything right. The fishermen watch to see how, when they're with Jesus, these same discouraged people discover new powers within themselves and walk away straight and well and ready to work.

And I can imagine when the fishermen have been with Jesus a while they are saying to one another, "We just have to watch Jesus if we want to know about God's wishes, and the kingdom of heaven."

Prayer: Thank you, God, for Jesus. Thank you for the people on whom he made such an imprint that they caught his spirit and passed on what he taught. Thank you for all the happiness that his birthday brings each year. May "thy kingdom come" in us as we find out how to show his love and helpfulness. Amen.

Leader: Today, when we read the stories of Jesus we feel as the people who knew him felt, and say with them, "It was a wonderful night when he was born!"

Long after Jesus lived people were saying it. They made songs about it, and put in lovely thoughts of angels, and songs in the sky, and a star that led Wise Men to him from far away.

Song: "The First Noel."

Offering and Christmas Music.

Each year in the church school whose Primary services of worship are here described, the children go for their Christmas service to a large room where a rug is spread on the floor, a fire burns brightly in the fireplace, and a large tree is twinkling with lights. They enter to music from the piano or from records like "Sheep May Safely Graze" or familiar carols. They gather on the rug in front of the Christmas tree for a program of poetry, music, song and story. Usually one class has been working on a special project which is summarized by them at this time by a dramatic presentation. One such service is typical, printed below:

Music, instrumental and songs, one about a Christmas tree.

Poem, "His Birthday" by Florence M. Taylor:

> When Jesus lived in Galilee
> He never saw a Christmas tree;
> He never saw the colored sheen
> Of tiny lights in evergreen;
> He never saw the wreaths of holly,
> The packages so gay and jolly;
> He just went on from day to day,
> And loved and helped in his own way,
> So long ago in Galilee,
> When Jesus walked beside the sea.
>
> I think he would have liked to know
> That we would keep his birthday so,
> With fun and jollity and cheer,
> With lights a-shining soft and clear;
> With friendly greetings 'cross the miles,
> With love, and kindliness, and smiles,
> With secrets and surprises gay,
> And joyous carols all the day.

I think he would have liked to know
That we would keep his birthday so.

Origin of Christmas Trees. (A child had asked the week before,
"Why do we have Christmas trees?" The second grade
teacher knew the story of Martin Luther's coming through
the woods and seeing a star over a fir tree, and bringing the
idea home. In 1947 a news item over the radio told of the
placing of a Christmas tree on the grave of the German immigrant who one hundred years before brought the idea to
America, and had the first Christmas tree here.)

Poems about Christmas trees by Annette Wynne:

The Fir Tree

I heard a mother fir tree say
All in the wood a summer day,
"Children, if you're straight and good
In the wood,
You shall grow at last to be
A Christmas tree!"

And oh, the small trees heard
Every single word,
And the little stars shone down to light
The limbs like Christmas night,
And so all year they stood
Straight and good;
And then we brought one here to be
Our shining Christmas tree.

Pretty Fir Tree

Pretty fir tree, when you grew
In the dark and damp and dew,
Did you ever dream that you
Would come and stand before our sight
Dressed in gold and silver light
On Christmas night?

141

Pretty fir tree shining so,
I am glad you learned to grow,
I am glad you came to be
Our Christmas tree.

Shine upon us all the night,
Fill our hearts with Christmas light,
Let us make our small place bright
All life through,
Pretty fir tree, just as you!

Songs: "Now sing we all merrily, Christmas is here"; "We wish you a merry Christmas."

Introduction to Dramatization: Christmas trees stand for Christmas and happy times. You told of other things that stood for Christmas in your minds last week (naming them).

We know what it means to have symbols, something to stand for an idea, or for something that has happened.

We have lighted candles to stand for all we are thankful for. We lighted one candle two weeks ago for Jesus. The third grade has been thinking ever since we all went to church of the imprint Jesus left on the people who came after him. They have used candles, too, and will tell you for what they stand.

Candle-lighting:

Large white candle lighted and held by John, who stood in front of the fireplace, the rest of the class in semi-circle, with blue candles, around him. *Introduction,* by John, explaining how the class had been deciding on what the thoughts and ideas and acts of Jesus were which had left an imprint. They had found some of them, and would let each candle stand for one, as a child lighted one after another.

First Child lighted her candle from white one, and said that it stood for the idea of sharing things more than had been done before. Told story of Rich Young Ruler.

Second Child: the idea that the most important people were those who serve others, and who help most. Told story of Jesus washing feet of disciples.

142

Third Child: the idea of doing good even to your enemies. Explained it is very easy to be good to your friends, quite different to do good to enemies.

Fourth Child: the new idea of God which Jesus gave, loving and like a father, instead of strict. (His word was "tough"—but he quickly added "only in a nice way.")

Fifth Child talked about numerous complicated laws boys had to learn and obey from the books. Told story of Jesus healing on Sabbath and being accused of breaking law. Candle stood for idea that people were more important than laws.

Sixth Child: candle stood for the courage which Jesus gave people. "My candle stands for the feeling Jesus gave people that they could do things."

Seventh Child followed up this idea, by telling story about one of the people Jesus healed, and lighted candle.

Eighth Child: the fact that Jesus had made people *want* to do right things—"not because they were made to do them."

Ninth Child: that our neighbor is anybody who needs our help, whether he happens to live next door or far away. Told Good Samaritan story.

Tenth Child: the Golden Rule, repeated it and explained it had been in the world long before Jesus came, but Jesus had liked it, and said it over again.

(After the semi-circle was completed the children stood a minute with lighted candles, then solemnly blew them out, and took their places again on the rug.)

Leader: It was because of all these things that he was called king, and even "king of angels"—the beings supposed to live with God. There is a song that calls him king of angels.

Song: "O Come, All Ye Faithful" (as children, to get a change of position, marched around the room).

Poem "Because He Came" by Nancy Byrd Turner:

> Because Jesus came,
> Every year on Christmas night,

Songs begin and candles glow,
And we talk, while stars shine bright,
Of a Christmas long ago.

And because he came
Hearts are kinder everywhere.
And the hungry and the cold
And the sad have better care
Than they had in days of old.

Another poem about an evergreen tree. (The poet, Edith Kent Battle, is talking to it.)

O evergreen upon the hill,
I see you from my window sill.
Your slender tip is pointing far,
As if it counted every star.
To find the one, like brightest gem,
That shone on little Bethlehem.
O evergreen upon the hill,
I think it must be shining still!

Leader: I couldn't begin to tell you all the poetry or all the pictures that have come into the minds of people thinking about Christmas, and what the first Christmas must have been like! The very first poetry was made by friends who knew Jesus, or whose friends knew him. In the stories they wrote about it they put the most beautiful thoughts they had, so they are like poetry as they are in the Bible.

Reading of Luke and Matthew stories (abridged).

Songs about the First Christmas: "Noel"; "Come Softly"; "Silent Night"; "I Heard the Bells."

Offering Service: Announcement about the number of "gardens" being sent through the Friends Service Committee.
    Trimming the tree with woolen gifts for "children who are cold."

144

A Christmas Prayer "We Thank Thee, God" by Frances Hill:

> We thank thee, God,
> For candlelight and spicy pine;
> For holly wreaths and stars that shine!
>
> We thank thee, God,
> For joy and peace within our land;
> For loving friends who understand!
>
> We pray thee, God,
> For children just across the sea
> Who may not have such gaiety.
>
> We ask thee, God,
> To help us find a way to share
> Our love with others everywhere! Amen.

TWO AFTER-CHRISTMAS SERVICES

I

"Christmas Is Magic"

Building on the children's happy recollections of Christmas and the Christmas season, and the second-grade's interest in a book called *Little Things*, this service was designed to arouse appreciation of the happiness little thoughtfulnesses can cause, and the desire to make the Christmas spirit operate all through the year.

Quiet Music: "The Earth Is Full of the Loving-kindness of the Lord"; "The Christ-child Is Born, Sing Allelujah!"; "Tell Me the Stories of Jesus"; "Quiet Our Minds."

Songs: "Come, Oh Come, Let Us Worship"; "The Christ-child Is Born."

Conversation: (Leader quoted someone who said he wished Christmas would last all the year, and asked why he should have wanted it. Children pointed out the impracticability of

145

this, as our homes would be continually cluttered up with packages. She quoted another person who said there was a sort of magic about Christmas, and asked why anyone should say that. One child said that at Christmas time everyone was good-natured, even in crowds in the stores, and even people who were mad at one another were kind to one another at Christmas. Someone else said that Jesus was magic. Leader said it seemed so sometimes, but that it was not magic that made us think that, and a child helped her out. It was because, he said, Jesus had so much kindness and love and friendliness. Another said Christmas could last all the year if everybody would be like that, and show friendliness all the time.)

Leader: Once children were thinking about why we come to this room in the middle of the morning, and their thoughts made a poem to remind us:

> Walk slowly, be silent,
> For this is the place
> Where loving and kindness
> Remind us of God.

Another second grade gave the thoughts and the tune for the verse we sing at the beginning of our services. As we make it our prayer now, let's think of all the places where we found loving and kindness during vacation. For that was a part of "the wonders He has done."

Prayer-Song: "Quiet Our Minds."

Quiet (for recalling things that brought happiness at Christmas).

Children's Responses

Introduction to Story of what made the leader happiest. It might have seemed a little thing to some, but children were asked to see if they could tell why it seemed a big thing to her. (On the table, in the center, was what looked like an ordinary little table Christmas tree, about fourteen inches

146

high. There were some silver threads on it, and a few little colored balls.)

She reminded the children of what a second-grade teacher had told the group about her trip to Austria in the summer; of the children she had seen, how little they had to eat or wear, and how the shops were empty of almost everything, so that even if people had money there was nothing to buy. Reminded them, too, of how Miss L—— had hoped we in America could build a "bridge of friendship" between here and Europe, and how many people had undertaken to "adopt" children over there, to whom they would write and send packages. Leader said many friends were giving her clothes and food all the time to send to children in whom she herself was particularly interested and told how Paula and her sister Anni, two Viennese children, were constantly writing her charming letters. Two of the letters had been used some weeks before in the second grade, to show how Austrian children celebrated Christmas. In response to those the leader had sent the girls a large illustrated card with "The Night before Christmas" on it, and now read their answers showing their delight in it. She read Paula's all through, and where the English was faulty, explained that Paula was far ahead of her, for she herself could not have written those words in German at all. The second letter, from Anni, contained a Christmas song in English which Anni's school class was learning, and the whole group sang it, the tune being familiar, and having so much repetition, it was easily sung:

> All the bells on earth shall ring,
> On Christmas day, on Christmas day,
> All the bells on earth shall ring
> On Christmas day in the morning!

Story: It was a week before Christmas. All the leader's packages for friends and relatives in different parts of the United States were wrapped and taken to the post office. Weeks before that the packages for the children in Vienna had been wrapped and sent off. But there had been a strike, and it was not certain that the Christmas presents would reach those far-off children in time. She was thinking of them, and hoping, hoping that the boxes of food and candy and clothes and toys would surely reach them. They had so little, and a box for Christmas would mean so much!

Just then the postman came to her door. In his hand was a long tubelike package wrapped tightly round and round with gummed tape. It had a foreign stamp on it and one which showed it had come by air. Leader looked and looked at it, the stamp, the writing, the address at the top. It was from the very children who had written those letters, one of them with the song in it. What could they be sending her?

"Oh dear," she thought, "I hope they have not gone out and bought me something, when they have so little themselves, and when, even if they have money, it is so hard to find anything in the stores! What *can* this be? A big, long, fat candle? But where would they get that? They haven't candles enough themselves, for the electricity goes off at a certain hour every day."

She put the package in the corner, standing it up. She wanted to unwrap it at once, but she made it a practice never to open her parcels before Christmas. But she kept looking at it. What *could* it be? She went over and weighed it in her hands again. It was good and solid. It didn't rattle; it made no sound. She smelled it. It had no smell except a sort of damp smell from the rain outside. She put it in the corner again, but she couldn't forget it. She kept looking at it. It seemed to be talking to her. She could almost hear it say, "Open me!" She began to think how she would feel if she had traveled five thousand miles, and then the person to whom she was sent didn't even unwrap her! She was sure she should want to be opened.

"But Christmas is a whole week away!" she said to the package.

"I know," it seemed to say, "but I've come from so far! Couldn't you just cheat a little?"

148

The more she thought of it, the more she was sure she ought to open it. She grew more curious about it every minute, and kept listening to what it certainly was saying to her.

"All right," she finally said, going over to the corner with a big pair of shears, "I *will* open you!" The big cylinder seemed to jump right into her hands, and she snipped away at all the gummed tape and tore off every bit of the paper.

Finally she had in her hands what looked like some Christmas greens, only they were all wound around something in the middle, with lots and lots of cord, to hold the branches together. Snip, snip, went her shears, until the string was all cut away. But the greens did not fall apart. She examined them. They were wired to something! Down at one end it was thick, where several stems were wired together. She bent the outside branches down gently, one, then another, then another, until they were no longer bound close, but were spread out—each one seeming glad to be bent down by the wire that bound them to the central stick, until they all seemed to be saying, "See! We're a Christmas tree! Paula and Anni went to the park and picked up little twigs from under the fir trees, to make me!"

The leader's eyes got bigger and bigger as she looked and looked. Yards and yards of wire and twenty or twenty-five clusters of twigs had been used to make this perfect little Christmas tree which the children here could see on the table. No, Paula and Anni had not bought a present from the stores; the only thing they had bought was a package of "angel's hair" which hung on the branches, and a little box of tiny white candles (which was too bad, for the leader did not know how to fasten them to the branches). So she hung on some little colored balls she had.

After the Story (and the children's amazed appreciation which included close examination of the tree) leader referred to the book *Little Things*, and said she felt like writing a Book of Little Things herself, after receiving the tree, and putting in the book all the ideas she could think up for making her

149

friends happy which wouldn't mean spending money, and which, like the tree, seem little, but which, as the tree had for her, might turn out to be big for others.

Offering (referred to the packages of seeds being sent to Europe and Japan; little things, to make eighty-one big gardens!).

Birthdays: (Six children went up to light candles for December birthdays, while Wendy, whose birthday was nearest Christmas, lighted the seventh for Jesus.)

Birthday Prayer: (That as these children grew in size and strength and knowledge, they would have more and more ideas for little ways to make people around them happy, and extend Christmas throughout the years.)

II

"HE WANTS ME TO DO IT"

This service was planned to lead from thoughts of Christmas to the "imprint" left on followers of Jesus whose work is seen today in centers of health, recreation, child care, education.

Quiet Music: Selected, then "America the Beautiful"; "The Fathers Built the City"; "The Earth Is Full of the Loving-kindness of the Lord"; "Maker of the Planets"; "Quiet Our Minds."

Chime Song: "Hark to the Sound."

Leader (quoted last line of this song, "Praise God for friends" and invited talk about how friends contributed to Christmas happiness.)

Prayer:
For all the acts of kindness we have seen,
For all the loving thoughts of people toward us,

For all the loving thoughts which we have had ourselves,
For everything that makes us wish Christmas would last,
Thank you, God. Amen.

Leader: All we have been saying about Christmas spreading
joy everywhere almost makes us feel that joy *is* everywhere;
that everyone is singing, "The earth is full of the lovingkindness of the Lord."

We know there are families who would not have thought
that. Some might even find it hard to believe God *is* kind,
and that there is love for everybody. Who would they be?
(Children mentioned European children and Chinese children suffering from war, and children anywhere who are
hungry and cold.)

There is a story that matches some of the thoughts we
have been having. It is not a true story, but you will see what
is true about it. There are three people in it, but they are not
named. They are really symbols: they stand for others. The
candles will stand for them, too. I shall light them as I tell
the story.

Story: He Wants Me to Do It. (*First candle lighted.*)

There was once a man who traveled about to see what he
could see and hear what he could hear. He saw the sunshine
and rain making food grow. He heard a father comforting
his children. These things made him think of God. He
thought about him a great deal, and the more he thought,
the better he understood what God was like. One day the
traveler came to a great and wicked city. The people in it
were so cruel that if they had ever known what goodness
and kindness meant, they had long ago forgotten it. Everywhere was misery. Everywhere was suffering. It made the
traveler sad and set him to thinking.

"God loves people too much to have this going on," he
said to himself.

"Somebody ought to show them that he does," he said to
himself.

Then a great thought came to him. *"He wants me to do it,"* he finished.

"The reason they make mistakes," he said, "is because they don't know about love. They need teaching."

So he began to teach those who would listen. Others tried to stop him. They made fun of him. They said people were supposed to be selfish and unkind, that God made them so. But the Teacher knew more about God than they, and he went on teaching. He started a school, and the wickedest ones grew frightened. They did not approve of learning and tried to tear down the school. But the Teacher went on teaching and he taught until he died.

Now the Teacher had a Friend who had learned from him about the love and goodness of God. [*Second candle lighted.*]

One day this Friend set out to see what he could see and hear what he could hear. He saw many sick with diseases. He heard children crying because they had no homes. It made him very sad and set him to thinking.

"God loves people too much to have this going on," he said to himself.

"Somebody ought to show them that he does," he said to himself.

Then the same great thought came to him that had come to the Teacher. *"He wants me to do it,"* he ended.

He began to study to find out the reason for people being sick, and why it was that some children had no homes.

The people said he was foolish. They said God must have wanted some to be sick and lame and blind and poor and others to be well and comfortable. But the Teacher's Friend knew more about God than they. He went on studying. He found that there were laws for keeping well and he learned some of them. He built a hospital where doctors and nurses helped the sick to get well and taught the well how to keep well.

The people still thought he was foolish. They said he knew enough already. But he kept on studying.

He found out why a part of the world had more than an-

152

other part, and he tried to teach people to be fair and share with one another. And he kept on studying and teaching and helping. He spent all his money building a great home. In it blind people were taught to read and the deaf and dumb to speak and understand. Little homeless children were brought there to live.

The Teacher's Friend, an old man now, died, sorry that there were still so many who were unhappy.

"God loves people too much to have this going on," were the last words he said.

Now there was a little boy named Tim who lived in the home which the Teacher's Friend had built. He was a thin, ragged, miserable little figure when a nurse found him, sick and alone. She lifted him in her arms and carried him to the hospital. When he was quite well, since he had no home, the Teacher's Friend took him to the home he had built, and there Tim lived, a happy, healthy, loving little boy.

One day Tim started out for a walk to see what he could see and hear what he could hear. He heard a child's loud cry. He ran to the corner and looked down the street. Some big boys were trying to snatch from a little child the handle of his roller coaster. The child was crying, but holding on tight to his toy. At last, with one final lurch, the boys managed to get it free and ran off with it. They did not even stop to notice that they had knocked down the child.

Now the Teacher's Friend had taught Tim much about the lovingkindness of God, and if the boy thought about anything now, as he watched, it must have been something like this:

"God loves people too much to have this sort of thing going on," and after a moment, "Somebody ought to show them that he does," and then, "*He wants me to do it!*" for he ran just as fast as his legs would carry him toward the unhappy child. [*Third candle lighted.*]

There was a little cut on the child's forehead. Blood was coming out. His cries grew louder and more frightened until Tim reached him.

"I'll take care of you," said Tim. "What's your name?"

"Billy," answered the child between sobs. "Those boys took my roller coaster. They hurt me."

"I saw them," said Tim, "that's why I came running. See, there's a drugstore. They always help hurt people in a drugstore."

He took Billy by the hand and together they went inside.

"He fell down and cut his forehead," explained Tim to the man behind the counter. "I told him you'd fix him up."

"Of course we will," said the man, and Billy's cut was bathed and bandaged before his tears had time to dry.

They thanked the man and went outside just as the big boys came back. When they saw Billy's bandage they stopped. Tim wondered if he dared tell them what he thought. They were bigger than he. They probably wouldn't pay any attention to him. Maybe they'd fight him and knock him down. But it wasn't fair, and they ought to know it.

He swallowed something in his throat before he could speak. Then he said bravely, "That's Billy's coaster. I saw you take it, and you knocked him down."

The boys laughed. "So what? He's a little crybaby. If he hasn't got spunk enough to hold on to his things, why, anyone that's strong enough has a right to take it from him."

"Not if it isn't yours," said Tim, his eyes blazing. "It isn't fair!"

"Aw—who cares?" answered the boy. "That's the way things are," and he went on with Billy's roller coaster. The older boy rolled up his sleeves ready for a fight.

By this time Billy didn't care if they pounded him black and blue. He knew he was right. He knew more that was true about the world than these boys did. He ran after the disappearing boy—and stood, firm, in front of him.

"That's *not* the way things are," he told the boy. "They needn't be! Come on! Give Billy back his coaster and say you were only fooling. It will make him like big boys better. He thinks they're all mean now. He'll think that's the way the world is."

154

The boy looked at Tim. "You're a funny one," he said. But he turned and went back. He winked at the other boy who pulled down his sleeves.

To Billy he said, "Here's your coaster, Bill. Thanks for the ride. We were only fooling, you know. Too bad you got knocked down. How would you like a soda?"

Billy's tearful face turned into one great surprised smile which meant, "Why, I thought big boys were mean, and they're *nice*! I like big boys."

Tim grinned at the big boy. Then he went whistling down the street to see what he could see and hear what he could hear.

(Responses to the story were spontaneous. Children enjoyed trying to guess the symbolism of the candles. Third graders thought the "Teacher's Friend" stood for Paul, others for the disciples, some for "kindness passed on."

Song: "The Earth Is Full of the Loving-kindness of the Lord" (as children took up offerings).

Prayer: God, Father of Jesus and of us, may our gifts and our acts really make others know that your world is full of lovingkindness. Help us to remember that you depend on us to show that it is true. Amen.

VIII

Music and Rhythms:
Their Contribution to Worship

In a two-and-one-half or three-hour church school session the need for relaxation and exercising of muscles at once becomes apparent. This might be met by a straight exercise or gym period. Such exercise may be boisterous and disorderly, lacking both inner and outer control and destroying much of what has been built up in the class and worship periods, or it may be one more medium through which appreciations may be deepened, ideas and feelings clarified through creative expression, and purposes strengthened.

EXERCISING TO MUSIC

In the church school about which we write the time set aside for relaxing and exercising has gone through stages of gymnasium "work-outs," games, folk dancing, and simple song practice, to become at last such a constructive and integrating part of the program that staff members wonder how they ever functioned without its help. In many ways the Music and Rhythms period contributes to the Service of Worship and often in the twenty-minute period itself, allotted to each class, there is worship inherent in the children's attempts to convey through movement an idea, an impression, a feeling about a person or a problem.

This does not happen every week with every group, but that it can happen as often as it does, and that what the staff calls "Rhythms" can provide a medium of expression into which every child can enter, which can be releasing and creative and even worshipful at times, makes one wish long sessions for every school, if only for the benefits of a Music and Rhythms period.

Classes at times still need strenuous "work-outs," but the music supervisor is quick to sense the atmosphere which a group brings with it and turn it to good account. We watch a restless class given a chance to bounce like rubber balls, run and whirl and use large arm-and-body movements. They are exercising, but they are doing it to music, to the rhythm of the piano. Their movements gradually become interpretive. The whirling children are leaves in autumn, stirred up and driven by the four winds; or they are apple harvesters, reaching up to the high branches of an imaginary fruit tree; or they are galloping horses, or snow shovelers, or ice skaters, until the edge of their energy is worn off, and they are ready to sit around the piano and practice a song, or listen to a poem which they can presently interpret with thought and feeling in a "rhythm."

CHILDREN'S IDEAS SET TO MUSIC

There is not always the need for such lively activity, however, and often the children come to the period with ideas of their own for which *they* direct the musical accompaniment. They are studying about baby animals: will the music leader make the piano sound like a kitten or a toad? Or another class has talked about the ways the seeds travel: will the piano please sound like seeds with wings, while the children become these, or tumbling puff balls, or cockleburs? (It is needless to say that the pianist must be versatile enough to enter not only into the children's feelings and experiences, but those of puff balls and toads as well.) Or couldn't they be The Friendship Train that is speeding across the country picking up at each stop carloads of grain for Europe? Or caterpillars, spinning cocoons and then coming out moths? Or birds flying south in the fall like the picture in the children's classroom?

POETRY AND SONG

The pianist combines poetry with the rhythms, and reads Rachel Field's "Something Told the Wild Geese" (page 215), and the children fly down the room in V formation as she first plays the whispering warning, and then the flight.

On other occasions she uses different poems (in this book, from her collection) or suggests the need of a tune for one, so that the department will have a new song for the service of worship. In this way she has drawn from the children tunes for litany responses and calls to worship, and for poems like "Heigh-ho for Snow," and the others at the end of this book.

PANTOMIME TO RHYTHM

A Migrant Worker's Day. A second grade has been thinking about the migrant workers. They would like, in the service of worship they are planning, to show what a long, hard, wearisome day the picker of their fruit has. To the rhythm leader they describe the day from the early rising to the final dropping on beds at night, and act out each bit spontaneously. Then they do it together, guided by the tempo of the music which the leader has caught from their description.

Indian Corn Dance. A third grade wants to play Indians. The music leader teaches them a corn dance: walking in a circle, looking at the sky and down at the earth (8 beats each, rhythm from drum); kneeling and planting seeds (8 beats); patting earth over seeds (8 beats); standing and in pantomime showing rain coming down from sky (8 beats); making circle with arms (the sun shining down on seeds, 8 beats); cutting the grown corn (8 beats); and walking in a circle again, arms high, looking at sky and earth (8 beats each). This corn dance becomes a part of the service of worship, Joel introducing it with the explanation: "The Indians thought of God in planting and growing."

Playground Swings. A second grade has made a play about a lonely child brought to a Neighborhood House. Their playground scene depends on action in swings. How can they swing without swings? With the music leader they work it out. The "pusher" stays in one place after each push (a chord on the piano). The swinger runs six steps forward and backwards, over and over—as the music does the same!

The Succoth. A visit to a neighboring Succoth Booth becomes more meaningful as the children, after hearing the stories connected with it, dramatize, in the rhythm period, the gathering of the First Fruits, building the leafy booth, bringing the fruit offerings. This is all done to a regular beat, harvesting the grain, reaching for fruit, putting it in imaginary baskets, marching with offerings to the booth.

These pantomimes are often woven into dramatic services of worship, and are done with seriousness and feeling.

RHYTHMIC MOVEMENT SIDESTEPS VIOLENCE

When certain scenes in the long story of the desert wanderings might be attacked too realistically, the regular beat of the music holds the children in check. The slave driver in Egypt never lays his hands on the slaves, but the upraised hand, lowered on the beat, and cringing of the

159

slaves give the same illusion with which the robber scene in the Good Samaritan story is enacted with no touching of the victim (with plenty of working off of energy, but no casualties).

Building the Walls. The building of the walls of Jerusalem in the Nehemiah story is done in this stylized manner, as a rhythm interlude in a dramatization.

In a several-act play of Zacchaeus Palestinian games are played in this way: ball-throwing, for instance, rhythmically, with no ball. Musical accompaniment, our music leader has shown us, takes care of many dramatic problems not met before. Pantomimic action tells the story with no learning of lines or self-conscious speaking. Only an announcer or narrator is needed. Sometimes this is a teacher, sometimes a child.

DRAMATIZING A SONG

The story of Brother Francis' crèche has been told, and the continental custom explained of villagers carrying lighted candles to the crèche in the church on Christmas Eve. In "Music and Rhythms" the children learn "Bring a Torch, Jeanette, Isabella," and, stationed in different parts of the room, holding imaginary candles, join the procession going to the church, singing as they go. Such a procession has sometimes been a part of the Christmas service of worship, but like many of the department's dramatizations, was worked out as a "rhythm."

APPRECIATION OF PERSONALITIES

Certain personalities lend themselves to expression in an art form, and St. Francis is one. Stories from his life are often told, showing his love for all living things, and in "Rhythms" we watch an eight-year-old boy portraying him. He seems, in the very way he walks through imagi-

160

nary woods to the gently played music, to have caught some of Brother Francis' spirit. He looks up at the sky as if at his friends the birds, then down, as the little animals gather about him. The children who are rabbits hopping about, or fawns, or wolves, rubbing their heads against him, seem to have caught his spirit, too, for there is no self-consciousness or fooling among them. This is not something directed by the music leader. It is the spontaneous expression of the children. And it seems to deepen the impression Francis made upon them.

We drop in on another third grade after the service of worship described in Chapter IV, on "The Man Who Talked with Flowers."

"It is very early in the morning," the pianist is saying, as she fingers the keys, and John who has evidently volunteered to be Dr. Carver, walks slowly back and forth. One or two little "animals" hop about, and some "birds" peep, to show they are waking up. Dr. Carver looks thoughtful. He stoops and picks a flower and studies it a long time. The music is like a whisper. He sits down. (His action is so realistic you are sure that seat is a stump.)

He continues to study the flower, as if he were asking it questions. The pianist watches, and when he stirs, makes the music louder and more dynamic. Dr. Carver has had an idea: he rises and hastens to his laboratory as the music follows fast. This pantomime could have been an effective part of the service of worship. Spontaneously and reverently acted here one still feels the atmosphere of worship.

NATURE RHYTHMS

Cycles. The box of yard-length cheesecloth scarves on the table invites "cycle" rhythms. It is fun to choose what season of the year one will be and find a scarf to match it, and then find one's place in the circle. For the seasons go "round and round" like the song, spring, summer, fall, winter, spring. As one skips along to the music one feels a part of a beautiful endless round, for the scarf held over one's head floats behind one, almost joining the next.

There is that Day and Night cycle, too. The black scarves with the gold stars are almost prettier than day's rainbow ones, as they float behind the bearers.

Growing. First-grade children like the "Growing" rhythms: the seeds, buried deep in the ground while the piano murmurs low music; seeds (and children) unfolding and growing as the music ascends, until at the top notes the seeds have grown to plants standing on tiptoe with branches reaching high.

Spirals. Second-grade children who have been fascinated by the spiral principle in uncurling ferns, in the winding pattern of the snail shells and the channeled whelk brought in from vacations, do spirals in finger painting while the music guides their widening circular strokes. Or they think of ways of acting out the spiral principle with finger, then hand, then large arm movements; and again, hands joined, winding themselves, as they march to the music, in what their elders would call a snake dance.

The pianist usually knows what the class interests are, for the teacher-supervisory conferences have enabled the supervisor to pass on the information. But the supervisor herself is often less prepared than the music leader for ways in which these interests may be originally expressed.

Stars. She is almost startled to find a third-grade group one day eagerly explaining to the teacher at the piano, "We're studying about the universe, and astronomy. Can we do the stars and the planets going around the sun, today?" She watches in wondering admiration as planets group themselves intelligently around the sun and begin

162

their rotations; she, who frequently has trouble remembering what goes around what, and which whirls as it goes. (Perhaps if, when she was eight, she could have taken an active part in the Solar System, she would now be more attuned to the music of the spheres.)

Crystals Formed to Music. Snowflakes have suggested many rhythms which, first worked out in "Music and Rhythms," have become a part of services of worship. In classes snowflakes have led to study and experimentation with salt crystals and sugar and alum.[1] There are many learnings from such a study, and with each one's wonder grows. An illustration of this is in what preceded a rhythm period where crystals were formed to music.

Let us sit in on a first-grade class and listen as Dorothy Ann, a mature eight-year-old daughter of an assistant in the department (and specialist in science), is sharing what she has learned from her mother. She is explaining the formation especially of those salt crystals in the saucers where the children stirred salt into water the week before, and which they now find, under the magnifier, to be perfect cubes, except as they were crowded out of shape. She tells how they formed from molecules, finding their places; how these are too small to be seen, but how each one fits into a pattern. She says that unless these are crowded or hurried they form perfect crystals. She takes up some bulbs from the table, explaining how they will not grow if they are crowded.

"It takes space for growing," she says, "and it takes a long time to make a crystal. Crystals need time and space for growing, just as you need time and space for growing."

"What *makes* these grow that way?" asks one puzzled child.

[1] Directions for carrying out such experiments are given in the Guide for Teachers accompanying the book *How Miracles Abound* by Bertha Stevens (Beacon Press).

"Well," says Dorothy Ann, "what makes you grow? What makes anything grow, the bulbs, the leaves, the flowers, the trees?" A child replies, "Why, food, and soil and sunshine and fresh air."

"But that doesn't make them *grow*," Dorothy Ann answers. "Soil doesn't make the chair grow, or the floor, or a building. There has to be something *inside* to make things grow."

The class teacher adds her voice: "That makes me think of the Bible verse song Miss Hardy taught us, 'O God, how wonderful are your works!'"

"Yes," says Dorothy Ann, in knowing agreement, "and 'Great things doeth He which we cannot understand.'"

In the rhythm period these children pretend to be molecules, floating around to the music until a chord brings them together in squares. They cannot quite make cubes.

But the snowflakes have no difficulty in the forming of their two-dimensional pattern. As suggested by Ruskin in his game, "The Dance of the Atoms,"[2] the pianist here suggests the children's whirling about in the air as vapor particles until they respond to the piano (or nature's) command: "To your places!" They discover at least two ways to form six-pointed snow crystals, and dance the rhythm over and over. Later this rhythm contributes to such a winter service of worship as described in Chapter V.

MORE SYMBOLISM

Good and Evil. A third grade reports to the music leader that they have been discussing the forces in them that seem to pull against each other. One, they say, is Conscience, telling them what to do; the other, the "bad" in them, telling them not to do it! They'd like to act that out

[2] *Ibid.*

164

to the music. Could she play "good" and "bad" music, using the treble and bass notes, while they, on two sides, pull against each other? They are up against the old problem of good and evil. At first they make of it a tug of war, but nothing is resolved. They have another idea. Evil is bound, and groping in the dark (black scarf!). In goodness and truth there is *freedom* to live and grow and act. There is more scope here for variation both in music and individual interpretation, and symbolism again of their own making.

CHRISTMAS CANDLES COME ALIVE

It is Easter time. Everything is coming alive. Song, painting and story carry the theme. Jane carries it to the third-grade rhythms when she suggests that they make their "Christmas candles come alive."

When the rhythm leader asks for ideas they recall the symbolism they attributed to the candles in their Christmas service,[3] standing for Jesus' teaching about loving our enemies, sharing with the poor, his story of "Who is my neighbor?" and his teaching about people being more important than laws.

Jane shows how she will stand as a candle at first, straight and tall, fingers meeting in a point high over her head. As the music plays, the hands gradually come down and spread, palms up. She seems to be taking in the whole world in her representing of "sharing."

In such ways the period for Music and Rhythms may become one not only of relaxation and exercise, but of creative opportunities, of artistic expression, and of spontaneous worship.

[3] Chapter VII.

The role of pianist or music leader in a children's department is an exceedingly important one. She is responsible for the songs taught, and the selection and interpretation of instrumental music used. The effectiveness of the service of worship is largely dependent on the atmosphere her music creates and her alertness in following the planned program or in quickly substituting one song for another, if such a shift is indicated.

In the more informal sessions if she can enter sympathetically and imaginatively into the children's world, and both follow and guide with improvisation, their chances for growth in worshipful attitudes is immeasurably increased.

It is due to such leadership through the years that the many values in Music and Rhythms have become apparent.

Part II

PRAYERS AND MEDITATIONS
LITANIES AND BIBLE VERSES
POEMS AND SONGS

Prayers and Meditations

O God, Giver of life and all that makes it good, we thank thee for health and strength and a chance to grow, for our homes and schools and friends, and for this church that speaks to us of thy love and thy call to help make a friendly world.

Help us all, through our study, worship and living together, to be more understanding in our minds, more loving in our hearts, and more ready to help in whatever ways we can. Amen.

AFTER THE SUMMER VACATION

God, we come here today from many different places, from many happy experiences. In our church school we are finding new teachers and new friends. Our minds are full of memories of the summer and plans for our winter's work.

Now we have come to this quiet place where each week we shall gather to think about you. We do not know very much about you, but we wonder about you and your world, and we can stop often to share our thoughts. May we learn to love the quiet here, and know we shall have new thoughts of you as we study your ways.

To this quiet place we have come again, God, to think about you and the days that have just passed.

For the fun we have had, we thank you;
For the kindness we have seen, we thank you;

169

For friends, and love and understanding, we thank you;
For the times we were brave, and for the times we had
    strength to do something hard, we thank you. Amen.

Whatsoever things are true, whatsoever things are hon-
orable, whatsoever things are just, whatsoever things are
pure, whatsoever things are lovely, whatsoever things are
of good report . . . think on these things. Philippians 4:8

PRAYER AFTER CHILDREN HAVE FOUND BEAUTY IN SNOW,
IN STONES, IN FLOWERS, IN FRIENDLINESS

God, Creator of all that is beautiful, you must love
beauty, you have put so much of it into the world! We see
it in the sparkling white snow, in the colors of stones, in
the sunset sky, in flowers, in friendliness. As this beauty
has come into our lives, help us to give it back to the world
in friendliness and thoughtfulness which others will find
beautiful. Amen.

MEDITATION ON PRECIOUS THINGS

Let us think of precious things that money cannot buy.
. . . (Responses from children). . . . *Thank you, God for
joys like these.*

Let us think of friends that love us, and the nice things
they do to make us happy. . . . (Responses). . . . *Thank
you, God, for joys like these.*

Let us think of ways in which we could show we love
them. . . . (Responses). . . . *Thank you, God, for thoughts
like these. Amen.*

AN OLD SONG OF THANKS

For the precious things of heaven, for the dew,
And for the deep that coucheth beneath,

And for the precious things of the fruits of the sun,
And for the precious things of the growth of the moon. . . .
And for the precious things of the everlasting hills,
And for the precious things of the earth and the fulness
    thereof. . . .
We give thanks unto thee, O God; we give thanks.
              Deuteronomy 33:13-16; Psalm 75:1 (A.S.V.)

Inside each of us is the part that no one can see or touch. It is the part of us that feels like singing when we are happy, and like crying when we are sad. It is the part that is lonely for friendship and love. It is the part that gets hurt when things are not fair and rejoices when they are made right. It is what thinks and feels and wishes. It is the part that goes on living after our bodies die.

It is the part of us which speaks to God when we pray the prayers which mean most to us. It is the part that is listening to God when we have our truest thoughts.

It is what people mean when they talk about one's spirit, and it is a part of God, for God is spirit.

God, whose spirit meets our own
    When we would call thee near,
Come to us, and speak to us,
    In the silence here.

Father of our spirits, in the quietness of this hour we make ourselves ready to speak with you. We know we

171

need not go to any distant place, or any special place to be with you. We have only to wish for your understanding and your love to find ourselves with you. We feel your steadiness; our thoughts come truer; our spirits rest in the sureness of your ways. May we feel your spirit near us now.

THE EIGHTH PSALM (Paraphrased)

O Lord, our Lord,
How wonderful thou art in the whole earth!
When I look up into thy heavens; and see the moon and
    the stars thou hast made
And know that some of those little stars are other worlds,
    and are many times larger than our world,
I think how small men and women and boys and girls seem!
Yet thou hast made them with hearts that love, and minds
    that think;
They are almost like thee, and thou dost love them.
Thou hast let them rule over thy great universe which they
    are learning to understand.
Thy children have learned to use many of thy glorious gifts;
Even the stars in the heavens are charted by them.
O Lord, our Lord, how wonderful thou art to us![1]

MEDITATION ABOUT LIFE

Let us think about Life:

The life in the seeds that grow into great trees;
The life in tiny shells on the beach,
Which grows and causes the shells to grow
To shelter the life inside;
The life in our little dog at home

[1] Source unknown.

172

That makes him jump up on us to greet us,
And makes him different from a toy;
The life in baby brothers and sisters
Whose laugh makes us laugh, too,
Who are too small to talk, and yet
Whose eyes still seem to speak to us.

Let us thank God for Life!

MEDITATION ON WHY PEOPLE OF MANY KINDS GO TO CHURCH

Some are happy: they want to sing songs of thanksgiving.

Some are sad and lonely: they want to find friends.

Some are worried: they think the minister will help them. They want to be reminded of other times when it has made them feel better to hear the minister, and listen to music, and look at beautiful symbols.

Some want to be quiet, and go over what has happened to them lately.

We could do that now . . .

MEDITATION, AND RESPONSES

Many, O God, are the wonderful things that you have done. If I were to count them, they are more than can be numbered.

You have put life into us all, and given us ways to protect that life.

You have created us with feelings, so that we may understand each other. You have made us able to choose between those things which will help and those which hurt. You have made us able to recognize courage and kindness and be thankful for them. May we remember now times when we have seen kindnesses done. (*Children invited to think in silence of something kind they have seen.*)

Responses

Bible Verse to conclude sharing of experiences: "We have thought on thy lovingkindness, O Lord," or "The earth is full of the lovingkindness of the Lord."

Song: "For the beauty of the earth. . . . For the love that from our birth. . . ."

AFTER A TRIP TO A SUCCOTH BOOTH,
AND STORY OF ITS ORIGIN

Leader: This is a song or Psalm from the Bible. It was made by people long ago. Nobody knows who sang it first —perhaps it was made by a whole group of people, like us. They were thinking of all they had to be thankful for. As I read it perhaps you will remember how they had escaped from their "enemies" who were holding them as slaves in Egypt.

O give thanks unto the Lord, for he is good. . . .
To him who alone doeth great wonders. . . .
To him that. . . . made the heavens. . . .
To him that spread forth the earth above the waters. . . .
To him that made great lights. . . .
The sun to rule by day. . . .
The moon and stars to rule by night. . . .
To him that led his people through the wilderness. . . .
Who remembered us in our low estate. . . .
Who hath delivered us from our enemies. . . .
Who giveth food to all flesh.
O give thanks unto the Lord.
His goodness endureth forever.

Psalm 136

Leader: Let us sing "Quiet Our Minds" and in the quiet

174

that follows, think of what *we* would put in a prayer of
thanksgiving . . .

LITANY MADE FROM CHILDREN'S SUGGESTIONS

> For earth and skies,
> Sunset and sunrise,
> > *We thank you, God.*
> For the rhythms of your world,
> For night and day,
> For rest and play;
> For sun and rain, and sun again,
> > *We thank you, God.*
> For food, and health,
> *For life itself,*
> > *We thank you, God.*
> For people all around the world,
> For friends, and love, and marriage,
> For homes and little babies,
> > *We thank you, God.*
> For You, Yourself, God and the ways
> We have of knowing you,
> > *We thank you, God. Amen.*

PRAYER BEFORE A STORY OF WAR VICTIMS

Great Creator of all life, and Father of us all, you have
put us in a world filled with good things: food to keep us
all from hunger, wood and stone enough to shelter everybody.

Spirit of Love, you have given us families and friends
to love us. You do provide "for our wants to be supplied."
As we hear today about children in other parts of the
world, help us to remember that it is not because you do
not care that they are without food and homes, but because wars took away what you provided, and that you

have to depend on people like us to share the food and love you meant for all. This is our prayer. Amen.

God, our Father, thank you for all the love and care you put into the world. Help us to think of ways to show your love and care to those who have not felt it as we have. Amen.

LITANY OF THANKS FOR WISHES THAT COME TRUE

"Many, O Lord, are the wonderful things that thou hast done!"
For thinking of *people*, and giving them life,
    We thank thee, O God.
For making them able to think and wish, and dream,
    We thank thee, O God.
For helping them make their wishes come true,
    We thank thee, O God. Amen.

The earth is full of the lovingkindness of the Lord. . . .
Bring an offering and come into his courts. . . .
Enter into his gates with thanksgiving,
And into his courts with praise.
                  Psalms 33:5, 96:8, 100:4 (A.S.V.)

OFFERING PRAYERS

O God, about whose lovingkindness we sing, we have brought our money gifts which have been given to us to use for others. Help us to be thinking how best we can make some other children happy with the presents we shall buy, so that they, too, will feel like singing, "The earth is full of the lovingkindness of the Lord."

God, Father of all children, we bring different kinds of gifts today. Money gifts are the easiest of all. Even toys are easy, for they are fun to make. But when we think of how much our friends mean to us, we know there is no gift that can be as important as our love and friendship. May we remember that what counts with those who receive our gifts is whether we really care about what happens to them, as Jesus cared. Amen.

PRAYER AT THE BEGINNING OF A "WORLD FRIENDSHIP" SERVICE

We thank you, God, for your love that reaches away around the earth, and yet is felt by each one of us in a special way as it comes to us through our families, our friends. We even feel it as a part of ourselves, and know that we, too, have a part in making it known and felt by others.

May our service here today bring us new thoughts, and true thoughts about ourselves as members of the great world family you love. Amen.

PRAYER BEFORE THE DRAMATIZATION OF THE
ZACCHAEUS STORY

O God, lover of us all, we have thanked you for the changes which love like that of Jesus can make. As we see acted out before us today the story of such a change, may we feel the power of that love, and know that it is in us, too. In the spirit of Jesus we pray. Amen.

O Lord our God, you are very great!
You can do wonders of many kinds.
You have made summer and winter;
You can bring about changes in nature,
Your love can make changes in people.

O Lord our God, you are very great!
And some of your greatness you have given to us,
To remind us that we can make changes in people.
May the story about to be told to us
Bring new thoughts to us
About your love, which is in us. Amen.

PRAYER AFTER A DRAMATIZATION OF WORK
IN A NEIGHBORHOOD CENTER

O God, we have seen how your love can change scowls
to smiles; how it can change sad days to happy ones. We
thank you for showing us the magic such friendliness can
work. May we find new ways, today, and other days, to
work such magic ourselves. Amen.

Thank you, God, for a world where we can depend on
certain things to happen if certain other things happen.
We belong to your world as truly as do the trees and the
flowers, the light of day and the stars of night. We have
seen friendliness follow friendliness as surely as the day
follows the night. We have seen unhappiness and misery
where unfriendliness was. We have seen love change peo-

178

ple's thoughts and acts as truly as the spring changes the frozen ground of winter.

God, Creator of the world, give us understanding, that we may know how to practice friendly ways which start friendliness in return. Amen.

Teach me, O Lord, the way of thy statutes; and I shall
    keep it unto the end.
Give me understanding, and I shall keep thy law; . . .
Make me to go in the path of thy commandments;
And quicken thou me in thy ways.

                      Psalm 119:33-37b (A.S.V.)

Thank you, God, for wondering—
For wondering leads to thinking,
And thinking leads to discovery,
And discovery leads to better living
When men find out that they can work with God.
Thank you, God, for wondering.[2]

LITANY INCORPORATING SECOND-GRADE
DEFINITIONS OF HUMANITARIANS

We thank thee, God, for great humanitarians:
For those who have loved other people so much they
would not let them go,
        We thank thee, God.
For those who have lighted the way for other lives,
        We thank thee, God.
For those who have had the spirit of helping,
        We thank thee, God.

[2] Source unknown.

For those who have put themselves in the place of others, and understood how they felt,

We thank thee, God.

For all those who have shown the same spirit that was in Jesus,

We thank thee, God. Amen.

BIRTHDAY "GROWING" PRAYER

God,
We praise thee for all growing things:
Plants and birds and little animals;
Grant that (we)[3] too may grow
Taller and stronger,
Braver and wiser,
Kinder and able
To do more for others. Amen.

PRAISE FOR A RAINY DAY

O God,
Giver of all good things,
We praise thee for rain in summer,
For coolness after heat,
For leaves washed clean from dust,
For hard soil made moist and soft,
For roots drinking in their food,
For the good scent of damp earth:
We praise thee, O Lord!

N. Simpson and L. E. Cox

Sometimes when I have said my prayer
And think I've finished with *Amen*
I keep on kneeling, waiting there,
Instead of standing up again.

[3] Or child's name.

I do not stir or say a word,
And yet I seem still to be praying
With thoughts instead of words, and feel
That God knows what I am not saying.

Verses from the Bible Which We Have Heard
in Our Services of Worship

When We Think about Coming to Church
I was glad when they said unto me,
Let us go into the house of the Lord. Psalm 122:1

When We Feel Glad
This is the day which the Lord hath made;
We will rejoice and be glad in it. Psalm 118:24

Thou hast put gladness into my heart. Psalm 4:7

When We Feel Like Singing
O sing unto the Lord a new song. Psalm 98:1

It is a good thing to give thanks unto the Lord,
And to sing praises unto thy name. Psalm 92:1

*When we think of caterpillars coming out of cocoons,
and seeds growing, and leaves changing color in the fall,
and how animals and babies grow, and how something
inside people makes them want to help others.*

Stand still,
Think of the wonders of God. Job 37:14 (Moffatt)

Great things doeth he, which we cannot comprehend.
Job 37:5

O God thou art very great! Psalm 104:1

181

This is the Lord's doing:
It is marvellous in our eyes. Psalm 118:23

This is the doing of the Eternal—
We can but watch and wonder. Psalm 118:23 (Moffatt)

Open thou mine eyes, that I may behold
Wondrous things out of thy law. Psalm 119:18

Many, O Lord my God, are thy wonderful works which
thou hast done . . .
If I would declare and speak of them
They are more than can be numbered. Psalm 40:5

The earth is full of God's lovingkindness. Psalm 33:5

Poems

Oh, it's nice to sit and think of things
  In summer's golden weather,
Of birds and flowers and children
  All in the world together. . . .

You can think of anything, very big and tall,
And never mind how big it is, even if you're small;
A child may think of things as great as anyone at all!
Annette Wynne

What Am I A Part Of?

Bigger and bigger and bigger:
Part of a mother,
Part of a family that loves you,
Part of a school,
Part of a church,
Part of a country,
Part of a universe.

I wonder—
How big is what I'm a part of?
I think
I shall never know
Jean Elliot (8 years old)

183

O God, I have to stretch my thoughts to think of you,
For you are great, as great as all the world,
And I cannot imagine all the world.
I can only understand the part I see,
And think, "Like that, and more of that, and more and
    more,"
Until it seems to go right on forever.
I stand on tiptoe and reach up and up,
Trying to see beyond the clouds and sky,
And think, "The world is taller still than that,
And God is greater even than the world!"

Firefly

A little light is going by,
Is going up to see the sky,
A little light with wings.

I never could have thought of it
To have a little bug all lit
And made to go on wings.

                        Elizabeth Madox Roberts

A Thousand Thoughts

A thousand thoughts come in my head
   And fill the livelong day;
Some are so big I wonder how
   They find the space to stay;
And sometimes they're so busy
   I go off quite alone
And talk to them beneath the sky
   Upon a mossy stone;
And I have quite a pleasant day

Just listening to what they say;
Some come from near and some from far,
And some are pretty as a star;
Some are quite big and some are small,
Some can't be understood at all
By just a child like me;
And so I'll wait until I'm big to see.

Annette Wynne

"How?"

How has God made so many flowers with no two kinds the
    same—
So many, many lovely ones I cannot even name?
How does he make a bumblebee, a snail, or butterfly?
How can he, just from tiny seeds, make trees to grow so
    high?
How do the plants know when to grow and how to come
    in season?
They never seem to get mixed up—I wish I knew the
    reason.
I've thought and thought about these things, but never
    understood:
It must be God is very wise, and wonderful and good.

Ann Codrington

I hold the bulb within my hand,
But it cannot understand
When *we* say, "It's time to grow";
And yet it knows; *how does it know?*

185

The Little Bird Upon the Tree

The little bird upon the tree
Knows more, far more, than you or me;
And no wise man could teach him how
To hang a safe nest from the bough,
And no wise man need tell him when
It's time to start down South again.

Annette Wynne

Co-operation

The bird helps the tree
   And the tree helps the bird,
And everything good
   Is "helping," I've heard.

For the bird helps the tree
   And the tree holds the nest,
Both do for the other
   Whatever is best.

And the bird gives its song
   And the tree gives its shade;
For helping each other
   All good things were made.

Annette Wynne

No One There

I like to think all by myself
   Of lovely, quiet things,
The falling snow, like lace of heaven,
   That shining winter brings;

The path of gold the sunlight makes
    Far out across the sea;
The quiet woods of tall, still trees
    With no one there but me.

Farther Than All the World

Farther than all the world
    Our little thoughts can go,
Farther than a railroad train
    In desert or in snow;

Farther than all the world,
    And ever and ever so high:
Deeper than diggers can dig,
    Higher than birds can fly!

Annette Wynne

Machines and Me

Machines have wheels and parts that work,
    Like bicycles and trains,
But they can't start themselves because
    They haven't any brains.

But I can ride my bicycle,
    And make it fast or slow,
And I can watch the lights and think
    When it is time to go.

And I can do a somersault,
    And I can make me walk,
Or run, or jump, or even swim,
    And I can sing and talk.

Machinery is wonderful,
  But I would rather be
A person that can think and move
  Than just machinery.
    Wouldn't you?

Thoughts and Words

It's very hard to find right words
  To say my thoughts for me;
If I could sing them, like the birds,
  How easy that would be!

For God is very wonderful—
  There should be words that sing
To tell my thoughts about his love
  For every little thing.

For all the great things, too—the sea,
  The mountains grand and high,
The stars, the clouds, and stormy winds
  That blow about the sky.

There must be lovely, starry words
  For thoughts of God like these;
Grand words, like organ tones, or waves
  Tossed up by restless seas.

The Bible songs have strange, old words;
  But I shall find, some day,
Clear, singing words myself shall choose
  For thoughts I want to say.

Edith Kent Battle

The Boy Jesus

I like to think that Jesus played
    And tumbled, wrestled, ran,—
That he was long a merry boy
    Before he was a man.

He once was just the age I am,
    And learned from teachers stern;
He long was just a thoughtful lad
    Before he taught, in turn.

I like to know he toiled beside
    His father at his trade;
His boyish fingers, calloused, bruised,
    Learned how things were made.

I like to think that Jesus planned
    Through long, long youthful years,
How he could help the helpless world
    And wipe away its tears.

It helps me understand him when
    I know he was a small
And gleeful boy, before he grew
    To be the Christ at all.

Earl Bigelow Brown

ORDER IN THE UNIVERSE

Order

The rule of good order
    Is nature's demand;

Fish swim in the water;
　Trees grow on the land.

When looking about us
　We know there will be
No gulls in a garden,
　No robins at sea.

All things are so ordered
　On earth by God's grace;
A place for all things
　And each thing in its place!
　　　　　　　　　Maud E. Uschold

Something Has To Come

Something has to come
　When you plant a seed,
Something has to come—
　A flower or a weed.

Nothing can stop it now
　That the sowing's done,
If need be, earth will quake
　So that it find the sun.

Nothing's strong enough,
　Darkness has no power;
Rocks shall burst apart
　For a seed to flower.

Tiny is the seed
　But God is its ally,

Who has the sun for magnet
To draw it across the sky.

Earth cannot contain
The fire of a seed,
Something has to come of it—
A flower—or a weed.

Annette Wynne

A Song of the Night

O Lord, my God, thou art very great;
Thou makest darkness, and it is night,
Wherein all the beasts of the forest creep forth,
And seek their food from God.
The sun ariseth, they get them away,
And lay them down in their dens.
Man goeth forth unto his work
And to his labor until the evening.
The earth is full of thy riches.
I will sing unto the Lord as long as I live:
Praise ye the Lord.

Psalms 104:1, 20-24, 33, 35 (A.S.V.)

O Beautiful Night

O beautiful night!
The dark is deep and far,
But in the bending sky
Shines many a star.

And each star pours its light
Upon our world below,
And each goes on its way
As it should go.

Safely they walk, those stars,
  Each shedding its light,
Telling the glory of God;
  O beautiful night!

Nancy Byrd Turner

Polaris

A falling star is a breathless wish,
  Gleaming through the night;
But lovelier is the constant star
  That guides men by its light
And shows the lonely shepherd where
  His slow flocks whitely roam,
And shines above the creaking mast
  To steer the helmsman home.

Frances Frost

The heavens declare the glory of God;
And the firmament showeth his handiwork.
Day unto day uttereth speech,
And night unto night showeth knowledge.
There is no speech nor language;
Their voice is not heard.
Their line is gone out through all the earth,
And their words to the end of the world.

Psalm 19:1-4 (A.S.V.)

The Stars

Look up at the night and see how high
And golden in the pure, dark sky,

Each quiet light, each perfect star,
Shines on us from afar.

Fair, faithful stars—so well they know
The long, lone way that they must go,
Each its own way that God has planned,
Above the sleeping land!

Look up at night and see them shine
Above this world of yours and mine,
While God, who guides them, long years through,
Guides us, his children, too.

Nancy Byrd Turner (slightly adapted)

A Litany of Lights

For lights that shine and lights that lead the way,
  We thank thee, O God.
For sun and moon and stars which are always in the sky,
  We thank thee, O God.
For lights on earth which man made with God's help,
  We thank thee, O God.
For the many living lights who try to shine like Jesus,
  We thank thee, O God.
For the light of God which shines in us,
  We thank thee, O God.

Primary Department, Hillside Presbyterian
Church School, Orange, N. J.

Maker of the Planets

Maker of the planets, hear our song to thee,
May this world of wonder follow thy decree!

Sun and moon and star-worlds ceaselessly obey;
May we heed thee faithfully as they.

Doris Gill

(See page 236 for music)

The Year Is Like a Rhyme

The lovely seasons roll around—
    The year is like a ring,
With roses after snowdrops,
    And summer after spring,
Then harvest-home, and slowly
    White winter drawing near,
And afterward, sweet April,—
    Oh, happy happy year!

No season ever failed us yet,
    Nor ever will, we know,
With violets and apple blooms,
    And golden wheat, and snow;
New color and new treasure
    For every single time—
Spring, summer, autumn, winter,
    The year is like a rhyme!

Nancy Byrd Turner

Over and Over Again

Over and over again
The seed makes the plant,
And the plant bears fruit,
And the fruit drops seed,
And the seed makes the plant,—
Over and over again:

It never begins, and it never ends,
Nothing is old, and nothing is new,
And nothing is ever lost.

Over and over again
The soil feeds the tree,
And the tree drops its leaves,
And the leaves make soil,
And the soil feeds the tree,—
Over and over again:
It never begins, and it never ends,
Nothing is old, and nothing is new,
And nothing is ever lost.

Over and over again
The clouds drop rain,
And the air takes it back,
And it forms into clouds,
And the clouds drop rain,—
Over and over again:
It never begins, and it never ends,
Nothing is old, and nothing is new,
And nothing is ever lost.

> Third Grade, Riverside Church

SPRING AND EASTER

For lo, the winter is past,
The rain is over and gone;
The flowers appear on the earth;
The time of the singing of birds is come.

> Song of Solomon 2:11, 12

While the earth remaineth, seedtime and harvest, and cold and heat, and summer and winter, and day and night shall not cease. Genesis 8:22

Words with Birds

What time is it, Robin?

What time is it, Thrush?

"The time when no berries
Are left on the bush;
When hills are all cold,
And boughs are all bare.
It's warm, farther south,
And we ought to be there.
But do not forget
Every year when we go,
That we'll surely return
Very shortly, you know."

What time is it, Sparrow?

What time is it, Wren?

"It's time we were back
At our business again.
Green has come on the hills,
Leaves are out on the boughs,
It is time every bird
Began building his house.
There are homes we must make,
There are songs we must sing;
It's the best time of all—
It is spring! It is spring!"

Nancy Byrd Turner

Spring Song

Spring is in the air today,
  I can feel it blowing.
    Something tells
    Me by the smells
That violets are growing.

God has rolled the blankets,
  The snow from off my flowers;
    Now on wings
    The bluebird sings,
In sun or shining showers.

Spring is in the air today,
  I can feel it blowing;
    Daffodils
    With golden frills
Springtime joys are showing.

               Jean Leathers Phillips

Today Is Spring

Though yesterday was winter,
  Today, today is spring.
The snowdrops opened wide the door
And crocus fluttered by the score,
All singing of the self-same thing—
   "Oh, yesterday was winter—
  Today, today is spring."

               Edith Lombard Squires

The Surprise of Spring

How did the south wind know it was spring?
How did it know that it was time to bring
Warm winds to coax out the flowers and trees?
    Who told the bees?

Who told the soft pussy-willows that grow
In fuzzy velvet coats? How did they know
Springtime was calling them, summer was near?
    I didn't hear!

I didn't hear that springtime was coming.
Only my heart started tripping and humming,
Only my heart sang: "Oh, springtime is here!
Springtime, the loveliest time of the year,
    Is here, is here!"

                              Catherine L. Barker

Spring Has Now Unwrapped the Flowers

Spring has now unwrapped the flowers,
    Day is fast reviving,
Life in all her growing powers
    Toward the light is striving:
Gone the iron touch of cold,
    Winter time and frost time,
Seedlings, working through the mould,
    Now make up for lost time.

Herb and plant that, winter long,
    Slumbered at their leisure,
Now bestirring, green and strong,
    Find in growth their pleasure;

198

All the world with beauty fills,
   Gold and green enhancing;
Flowers make glee among the hills,
   And set the meadows dancing.
                              Ancient Latin Hymn
         (Sung to the tune originally used for it,
            but afterward used for the Christmas
            Carol, "Good King Wenceslas")

Planting Time

Springtime is planting time.
   The fields are warm and clean.
The sun is bright, the wind is light,
   And leaves are growing green.

Springtime is planting time.
   Across each fertile hill
Planters must know what best will grow,
   And plant there what they will.

Springtime is planting time.
   The planter must allow
For toilsome ways till harvest days,
   And do his planting now.

Springtime is planting time,
   And when its day has flown
The autumn field will surely yield
   What springtime's hands have sown.
                              Clarence E. Flynn

Of All the Wonderful Things I Know

Of all the wonderful things I know,
The most wonderful is how a seed will grow;
How it lies all winter long,
Down where there is never a song,
All in the dark
And no one brings even a candle-spark;
And never a one comes to tell
That presently all will be well;
But however lightly comes spring the seed knows
And lifts its head and grows . . .

Of all the wonderful things I know
The most wonderful is how a seed will grow.

Annette Wynne

Do You Know? Have You Heard?

Do you know
The story of the seeds—
How leaves and branches grow?

Have you found
The secrets that the seeds keep
In the dark underground?

Have you heard
The tale of wonder
That the seeds tell without a word?

Daffodils

I love daffodils,
I love narcissus when he bends his head,

I can hardly keep March and springtime and singing
Out of my rhyme of song.
Do you know anything about spring
When it comes again?
God knows about it while winter is lasting.

Hilda Conkling

A Litany of Thanks for Waking-Up Time

(Read by one member of the group, with response, after
each line, "Father, we thank thee" except for last line, for
which response is indicated)

For the grass that grows greener each week . . .
For the crocuses pushing their heads through the grass,
    and the pussy-willows with their gray coats . . .
For the gentle rains and sunshine that are making things
    grow . . .
For the bursting buds we see on every tree. . . .
For all of Nature's waking-up . . .
For robins and their fresh spring song . . .
For our eyes, which see the beauty all around . . .
For hearts that know that God is in it all,
We thank Thee, thank Thee, Father.

Anonymous

A Prayer in Spring

God, Maker of heaven and earth and all that is in them,
we do not know all of your wonders, but we are learning
more day by day. Spring is full of them. All around us we
see what seemed to be dead living on in a new life. Thank
you, God, for life which goes on and on. Amen.

201

Beautiful Easter

O Easter, beautiful Easter,
This is the message you always bring:
Life, new life, for the trees and flowers,
The world, the people and everything!
Nothing can die forever and ever,
For all is God's and he holds it dear,
Easter, beautiful Easter,
This is your message every year!

Nancy Byrd Turner

Easter

The world itself keeps Easter day,
    And Easter larks are singing,
And Easter flowers are blooming gay,
    And Easter buds are springing.
            Alleluia!

John Mason Neale

The world itself keeps Easter day,
    And voices gay are ringing,
To tell to people everywhere
    The joy the season's bringing.
            Alleluia!

Anonymous

A Spring Litany of Rejoicing

We thank you, God for the signs of spring all about us;
    We thank you for all reminders that nothing is lost in
the world you have made;

That life goes on in one form or another.

Rejoice! Rejoice!
Rejoice, give thanks and sing!

We rejoice that the little grub can change to a beautiful dragon fly:

Rejoice! Rejoice!
Rejoice, give thanks and sing!

We rejoice that in the gray cocoons of the Polyphemus moth we can feel life, and know that a beautiful moth will come out, where a caterpillar went in:

Rejoice! Rejoice!
Rejoice, give thanks and sing!

We rejoice in your ways: we are thankful that there is a law of life that brings about change and growth. We rejoice that you care for life and want it to go on. It makes us feel safe. We know that whatever happens to us, we are in your loving care. Amen.

Easter Surprises

Out of an egg comes the singing bird;
    Out of a seed comes the flower,
Dark of the night turns to morning light,
    Clouds turn to snow or to shower.

Look for the wonders of Easter time,
    Wonders that April will bring,
Open your eyes for a new surprise!
    God is at work in the spring.

                Edith Lovell Thomas

If you tip back your head
And look up high
You will see the sun
In the wide blue sky
So bright that it makes you
Blink your eye.

If you bow your head
And look around
You'll see little live things
All over the ground
Coming and going
Without a sound.

If you stand quite still
Looking here and there
At the birds and the bees
In the warm spring air
You will find the summer
Everywhere!

Verna Hills

Shells in Rocks

I've been along the quarry road
    And I have watched men digging wells,
And everywhere it was the same—
    The stones were full of little shells.

And they are packed away in rock;
    They're under sand and under clay:
And someone said that they were left
    When the ocean went away.

I saw them in the stones that make
  A church, and in a bridge.
They're hidden in the solid rock,
  But they show along the edge.

You see them in foundation stones;
  They show in cracks and waterfalls;
And once I saw them on the jail—
  More little shells in walls.

We walk on them when we walk on roads;
  And they're packed under all the hills.
Suppose the sea should come back here
  And gather up its shells!

                              Elizabeth Madox Roberts

Thinking about Water

Let's consider water;
  Let's be thinking how
Without water there would be
  No leaf on any bough
(And that leaves make forests);
  How no flowers could bloom;
Not a daffodil, a rose,
  An aster's purple plume.
How there would be no apples:
  That wheat couldn't grow,
(And then what would we do for bread?)
  No bird be singing; no
Child laugh; no artist paint;
  No poet could write a song—
Why, all that's beautiful and fine;
  That's wonderful; that's strong

Depends on water. Water's life!
  Come, let's take a drink,
And while we satisfy our thirst,
  Let us stop and think!

Edith Romig Fuller

A Song of Thanks for Water

Praise ye the Lord.
He sendeth forth springs into the valleys;
They run among the mountains;
They give drink to every beast of the field;
The wild asses quench their thirst.
By them the birds of the heavens have their habitation;
They sing among the branches.
O Lord, the earth is full of thy riches.

Psalm 104:10-12, 24 (A.S.V.)

Sing praises . . . unto our God,
Who covereth the heavens with clouds,
Who prepareth rain for the earth,
Who maketh grass to grow upon the mountains. . . .
He causeth his wind to blow, and the waters flow.

Psalm 147:7-9, 18 (A.S.V.)

Stand still,
  think of the wonders of God.
When God works, do you know how?—
  how he makes lightning flash from the clouds?

Do you know how the clouds are poised,
that pour a deluge when it thunders?
                    Job 37:14-16 (Moffatt)

Rain

It gently falls in sunburnt places,
And wets the flowers' lifted faces.

It soaks the garden through and through,
And makes the meadow shine like new;

And feeds the roots of thirsty trees,
And ripens clover for the bees.

It swells the spring, the pond, the rill,
Where weary cattle drink their fill;

And makes a little sparkling pool
For dusty sparrows, clear and cool.

So, blessing flower and fruit and grain,
And man and beast, on hill and plain,
Falls God's good rain.
                        Nancy Byrd Turner

A Thank-You Prayer for Water

His showers cause the trees to grow, the flowers, and the
    grass.
  *The Lord hath done great things for us, whereof we are
      glad.*
His waters form the oceans, the rivers, and the lakes.
  *The Lord hath done great things for us, whereof we are
      glad.*

And water makes our engines go; it runs some big
machines.
The Lord hath done great things for us, whereof we are
glad.
There's water in our motor cars that help us get about.
The Lord hath done great things for us, whereof we are
glad.
His rains cause vegetables to grow; we need them for food.
The Lord hath done great things for us, whereof we are
glad.
The animals that give us meat and those that give us milk
Must have their water, too, or else they wouldn't even live.
The Lord hath done great things for us, whereof we are
glad.
We wouldn't even be, ourselves, if this great gift were
gone,
For water keeps us all alive, We need it, every one.
The Lord hath done great things for us, whereof we are
glad.

A third-grade weekday group

A Wonder Litany

(Made from the comments of children who had watched
the caterpillar cycle)

O God, how wonderful are your works!

We watch the caterpillars, and wonder:

They came from tiny eggs laid on a leaf.
When little worms came wriggling out
They ate the leaf and found in it
The very food to make them grow.
How is it moths and butterflies

208

Are given so much sense to know
On just what leaf to put their eggs?
    [Refrain (sung, see page 231 for music):] O God, how
        wonderful are your works!

And how can caterpillars make
Cocoons that are so small and tight?
    [Refrain:] O God, how wonderful are your works!

We're full of wonders in the spring,
How seeds can grow, how birds can sing,
How God can see to everything!
    [Refrain:] O God, how wonderful are your works!

We wonder too about ourselves:
How could God make people?
How could he teach them how to think?
How did the first ones ever know
The things we have to know, to live?
    [Refrain:] O God, how wonderful are your works,
        How wonderful are your works!

    Lovely moth emerging
        From your grayish pod,
    You make me think of birth, and death,
        And life, and change, and God.

A Tiny Egg

A tiny egg once held a germ
That grew and grew into a worm;
The worm grew bigger than its skin,
And left the shell 'twas living in;

209

And still it grew, until it spun
A chrysalis. *Still life went on.*

For from the chrysalis there came
New life, but changed in form and name.
With fluttering wings of beauty rare
A butterfly rose in the air.

The worm it once was could not guess
It ever would wear such a dress,
For born within those tiny germs
Is life beyond the dreams of worms.

Caterpillar, Caterpillar

(For use after the experience of studying or watching the
changes in the moth or butterfly life cycle)

Caterpillar, caterpillar, crawling on the ground,
Who has shown you where the leaves for your food are
found?

Caterpillar, caterpillar, growing as you feed,
Tell me how you know when you have eaten all you need.

Caterpillar, caterpillar, spinning in the air,
Whence came all those silken threads you are winding
there?

Caterpillar, caterpillar, how I wonder how
You could make the cradle snug where you're sleeping
now!

Caterpillar, caterpillar, what is telling you
As the days and weeks go by, when your sleep is through?

Caterpillar, caterpillar, I can feel you stir,
Pushing, breaking through the cradle where you were!

Caterpillar, caterpillar, crawling, sure and slow,
Out into the world again, *what has changed you so?*

Lovely, lovely creature, with your shining wings—
Caterpillar! You have filled me full of wonderings!

AUTUMN

Autumn Leaves

The red leaves are falling,
  The gold leaves and brown,
And their shadows with them,
  Drifting down.

To make a blanket, rich and deep,
Over the flowers fast asleep;
Humming a lullaby, sweet and low,
"Sleep little flowers—soon the snow

Will spread its beautiful counterpane
Above you, till the warm spring rain
Taps at your door and murmurs, 'Wake,
Rise and bloom for beauty's sake.'"

The red leaves are falling,
  The gold leaves and brown,
And their shadows with them,
  Drifting down.

                                    Marion Doyle

In October

There's not an earthly artist
    With all his paints and brushes
Can put into a picture
    The color of these bushes,
The beauty of these branches,
    The blueness of this sky.
No painters ever do it
    However hard they try.
Only the first great Artist
    The God who made us all
Knows how to make this color
    Each lovely, shining, fall.

                    Nancy Byrd Turner

Seeds

"Where are you going, you milkweed seed,
    Tilting along through the air?"
"I'm riding the winds till I find a home,
    Is there room in your meadow to spare?"

"Where are you going, you cockle bur,
    Riding along on my dress?"
"I'm stealing a ride to my next summer's home,
    I'll stop by the roadside, I guess."

"Where are you sailing, you maple tree seed,
    In your little green aeroplane?"
"I'm hunting a place to set out a tree
    That will grow in the sunshine and rain."

"Holly-hock, why do you spill out your seeds
  And let them fall down to the ground?"
"Oh, that is the way Mother Nature and I
  Set holly-hock plants all around."

"Cocoanut, why do you roll down the bank
  To the swift moving river below?"
"I carry a seed in my watertight coat,
  And will drift to a shore where 't will grow."

"Where are you going, you tumble-weed,
  Tumbling over the ground?"
"I go with the wind, and I turn somersaults
  To scatter my seeds around."

"What do I hear from the bush over there,
  That sounds like the pop of a gun?"
"I'm a witch hazel seed, and I shoot myself out
  And fly through the air—and it's fun!"

Seed Song

I've found seeds with silver sails,
Seeds with gauzy wings; with tails;
Seeds with little claw-like feet;
Some all straggly, some *so* neat:
But oh, a seed of any kind
Can start a wonder in my mind—
To *think* that such a tiny thing
Can hold within its covering
All the beauty of the spring—

Or material for a dress,
Waiting for the spinner;
Or in its little dark recess,
A vegetable for my dinner!

Marion Doyle

The Last Word of a Bluebird

As I went out, a Crow
In a low voice said "Oh,
I was looking for you
To tell Lesley (will you?)
That her little Bluebird
Wanted me to bring word
That the North Wind last night
That made the stars bright
And made ice on the trough
Almost made him cough
His tail feathers off.
He just had to fly!
But he sent her Good-bye
And said to be good,
And wear her red hood,
And look for skunk tracks
In the snow with an axe—
And do everything!
And perhaps in the spring
He would come back and sing."

Robert Frost

A Seed

A white-winged seed goes sailing by,
And mounts on breezes toward the sky,
I wonder what that seed will be,

214

A reed, a flower, or a tree?
A tree whose limbs are spread around
And casts dark shadows on the ground,
A flower with nectar in its cup
Where honey bees may come to sup,
A reed beside a quiet lake
Where green-winged teals their nests may make?
But whether flower, tree, or reed,
A thought of God is in that seed.

Milly Ruth Turner

Something Told the Wild Geese

Something told the wild geese
    It was time to go.
Though the fields lay golden,
    Something whispered, "Snow."

Leaves were green and stirring,
    Berries, luster-glossed,
But beneath warm feathers
    Something whispered, "Frost."

All the sagging orchards
    Steamed with amber spice,
But each wild breast stiffened
    At remembered ice.

Something told the wild geese
    It was time to fly.—
Summer sun was on their wings,
    Winter in their cry.

Rachel Field

Winter in a Psalm

He giveth snow like wool;
He scattereth the hoar-frost like ashes.
He casteth forth his ice like morsels.

Psalm 147:16, 17 (A.S.V.)

Snow Stars

The air is full of flying stars,
    The sky is shaking down
A million silver stars of snow
    On wood and field and town.

Frances Frost

A Prayer of Thanks For Winter

Let us thank God for winter:
For rime on the twigs, and for soft-falling snow;
For sunshine, and winds that set faces aglow;
For frost, and the frosty stars bright overhead;
For fires, and thick coats, and a warm cosy bed,
        We thank thee, O God.

N. Simpson and L. E. Cox

Song of the Snowflakes

It isn't only the flakes that fall
On the street and roof and all,
All the day and evening hours,
But white and shining stars and flowers.

A million, million tiny stars,
Dropping from the cloudy bars,
Falling softly all around,
On my sleeve and on the ground.

216

A million, million flowers white,
Falling softly day and night—
But not a leaf or stem, at all—
It isn't only flakes that fall.

Annette Wynne

Quiet Things

There's nothing quite so still as frost,
   Nothing so soft as snow.
Silently winter builds a bridge
   Where small streams flow.
Silently the thin smoke curls,
   Tenuous and blue,
Where love makes safe and warm
   A dwelling place for you.

Silently the little lights,
   Like fireflies through the town
Shine in friendly windows
   As the night comes down.
Summer comes with song, but these
   Are very quiet things:
Frost pictures on the window pane,
   The snow's white wings.

Louise Driscoll

Thanksgiving for Snow

The snow, the snow, the lovely snow
   Comes in the night.
It falls on street and hill
   Gentle and pure and white;
On field and valley and height
   Silent it lies and still.

And every growing thing
Fairer will be in spring
  And every frozen rill
Fuller at last will flow,
  Because of this good snow—
These flakes so soft and light
Drifting down through the night
  On the dark world below.
Thank God for such a lovely gift
As snow!

                          Nancy Byrd Turner

The Snowflake

Before I melt,
Come, look at me!
This lovely, icy filagree!
Of a great forest
In one night
I make a wilderness of white;
By skyey cold
Of crystals made
All softly, on
Your finger laid,
I pause, that you
My beauty see:
Breathe, and I vanish
Instantly.

                          Walter de la Mare

To a Snowflake

What heart could have thought you? . . .
Fashioned so purely,
Fragilely, surely, . . .

Imagineless metal
Too costly for cost?
Who hammered you, wrought you?

God was my shaper,
He hammered, He wrought me
From curled silver vapor, . . .
Thou couldst not have thought me!
So purely, so palely,
Tinily, surely,
Mightily, frailly
Ensculped and embossed,
With his hammer of wind and his graver of frost.

Francis Thompson

Snowflakes

On the tree
Jewelry,
On the pond
Diamond,
On the glass
Flowers, grass . . .
So the snow,
Swirling low
Scatters form
From the storm;
Every flake
New of make,
Every star
Singular.

Dilys Laing

Christmas Once More

There's a candle,
Red and glowing in a window,
And a ribboned wreath with bells
Upon a door.

There's a tree,
Green-branched and lighted in a corner,
And secrets wrapped in splendor
On a floor.

There's a sound of carols,
Clear against the darkness,
And a gleam of silver stars
From heaven's store.

There's a night, expectant,
Waiting with its children
To welcome Christmas peace and joy
Once more.

James Tippett

A Christmas Prayer

God of love, Father of Jesus and of us,
You seem very close to us at Christmas time.

We find you on every hand—
In the love of friends

220

Planning for each other's joy;
In the special thoughtfulness
Of people one for another;
In our own feelings of good will
Which would take in the whole world;
In the wish in our hearts
That everyone may have
His needs supplied
And be as happy and content as we.

The Brightest Gleam

The brightest gleam that ever shone
   Across the dark world's night
Was not reflected from the throne
   Of selfishness or might.

Nor was the torch that led the way
   To any diadem,
It was Love's gentle, golden ray,
   The star of Bethlehem.

The light that longest shall abide
   Among the distant years,
And have on weary faces dried
   The most of human tears,

Is not the glow reflected far
   From splendor's gleaming gem,
It is the light of one lone star,
   The star of Bethlehem.

Clarence E. Flynn

The Christmas Story

We'll set a candle, burning bright,
   Upon the window sill—and then
We'll read, beside its circled light,
   The story, once again. . . .

The story of the little town,
   The humble stable, dark and chill,
The angel's song that drifted down
   Above the pasture hill.

And while the Christmas story tells
   Of Wise-men, riding from afar,
Almost. . . . we'll hear the camel bells. . . .
   Almost, we'll see the Star!

Nancy Byrd Turner

The Bethlehem Children

Do you suppose the children
   Of little Bethlehem
Went in to see the Christ-child,
   And thought he smiled at them?

I think they must have loved him,
   And that no doubt each day
They tip-toed in to see him
   Between their work and play.

Perhaps they brought him presents,
   And tried with loving care
To help his mother, Mary,
   Like you, if you'd been there.

222

I'm sure they all remembered,
　　And as they older grew
They thought of him and wondered
　　How he was growing, too.

Edith Kent Battle

Indian Christmas

Pomegranates, guavas sweet
We will bring you for a treat,
Custard apples, plantains, maybe,
For your birthday, Jesus baby.

We will bring a garland gay
Dangling blossoms for your play—
You will love the colors bright,
And the scents for your delight.

Shall we bring a little cape
With tasseled hood of cunning shape
Would you like, if you could choose,
Little red and turned-up shoes?

Twinkling anklets for your feet—
Will they make your joy complete?
Will you sometimes let us, too
Play with gifts we bring for you?

Margaret G. Hammaker

What Shall I Give to the Child in the Manger?

What shall I give to the Child in the manger?
　　What shall I give to the beautiful Boy?
Grapes I will give to Him, hanging in clusters,

Baskets of figs for the Child to enjoy.
  Tam-pa-tan-tam, when the figs will have ripened,
  Tam-pa-tan-tam they will add to His joy!

What shall I give to the Child in the manger?
  What shall I give to the beautiful Boy?
Garlands of flowers to twine in His fingers,
  Cherries so big for the Child to enjoy.
    Tam-pa-tan-tam, when the cherries have ripened,
    Tam-pa-tan-tam, they will add to His joy!

Spanish Carol

The New Year

The year ahead—what will it bring?
At least we may be sure of Spring.

What will they hold, the coming hours?
At least we may be sure of flowers.

Blossoms, birds and budding trees:
Thank God! We may be sure of these.

Lord Balfour

MISCELLANEOUS

I See a Great Round Wonder

I see a great round wonder rolling through the air.
I see the shaded part on one side where the sleepers are
    sleeping,
And the sunlit part on the other side.
I see the curious, silent change of the light and shade

And distant lands as real and near to the inhabitants of
    them
As my land is to me.

Walt Whitman

Nations, Play Your Anthem

Nations,
Play your anthem,
But play it sweetly,
And above all,
Play it together.

Jennie Czekala

Every Day

So many things to do today,
    In city and field and street,
People going everywhere
    With quickly hurrying feet!

Some are plowing and sowing seed,
    And some are reaping grain,
And some who worked the whole night through
    Are coming home again.

Over the hill the shepherd goes,
    While in the busy town
People and carts and motor cars
    Are running up and down.

And everywhere they come and go
    In sun and rain and sleet,

That we may have warm clothes to wear
And food enough to eat.

Mary Osborn

My Song of Helpers

I have many helpers
  Who work for me each day—
At home, at school, asleep, awake,
  At work or at my play.

The baker is a helper,
  He bakes good loaves of bread,
Cookies, cakes, and crackers
  That children may be fed.

The grocer is a helper,
  He sells us sugar, spice,
Flour and vegetables,
  Fruit and eggs and rice.

The miller is a helper.
  He grinds the grains of wheat
To make the flour that children
  May have good bread to eat.

The farmer is a helper.
  He plants his fields with wheat,
Grows vegetables and fruit trees,
  Good food for us to eat.

I'll sing a song of helpers
  Who help me every day,

And work for me so willingly
In every, every way.
Eleanor Prince

Hospitality

If there comes to you a stranger
Who is weary, who is hungry,
Sore beset by evil spirits,
Seeking for a place to rest in,
Seeking for a place of shelter;
Give him of your food and garments,
Give him of your love and friendship,
Make a place within your wigwam
Where he, too, may find contentment,
Send him forth, with strength and gladness
In his mind and in his body;
That your life may be remembered
By the Father of Creation,
And your waking hours more pleasant,
And your sleeping be more restful,
That your days shall be the longer
In the Land of the Ojibway.
Ojibway Indian Code of Hospitality

Litany: The World Brotherhood of Workers

Let us remember the workers of the world.

For all who work to give us our daily bread: for the laborer in the field, and the farmer in the mart:

We thank thee, God.

For those who toil in the burning sun gathering the vegetables and the fruit we eat:

We thank thee, God.

227

For those who bring our food across the seas; for the
helmsman at the wheel, the sailor on the deck, and the
stoker in the hold:

We thank thee, God.

For all workers who unload our ships, who labor through
the night, who drive the rushing trains, who bring to our
door the food which helps us to grow:

We thank thee, God.

Unseen

I asked a little boy who cannot see,
"Then what is color like?"

       "Why, green," said he,
Is like the rustle when the wind blows through
A forest. Running water, that is blue;
And red is like a trumpet sound, and pink
Is like the smell of roses, and I think
That purple must be like a thunder-storm;
And yellow is like something soft and warm;
And white is pleasant stillness when you lie
And dream."

    "Then what is beauty like?" said I.
"Oh," said my little comrade who is blind,
"Beauty is like a voice that's dear and kind."

        Author unknown

Have You Heard the Music?

Have you heard the rain's soft music
 On the grass, and on the leaves,
 On the overhanging eaves,
While the wind, the music-master,
Calls the tune, now slow, now faster?

228

Have you heard the music
Of the wind and rain?

Have you heard the sunrise chorus?
Cardinals and bluebirds singing,
Mockingbirds and thrushes flinging
Joyful praises to the dawn
When the shadowed night is gone?
Have you heard the music
Of the birds at dawn?

Edith Kent Battle

A Music Litany

(Refrain from Beethoven: "Rejoice! Rejoice! Rejoice, Give
Thanks, and Sing!")

O God, from whom come the gifts of melody and song:
We give thanks for the music in the world:

For the music in nature,
In the song of birds,
And the hum of insects;
The music of the wind in the trees,
And the ripple of waterfalls:

Rejoice! Rejoice! Rejoice, give thanks, and sing.

We give thanks for the instruments of music, which
bring us sweet sounds through wind and strings;
And for the song itself, by which each of us can sing
our tunes:

Rejoice! Rejoice! Rejoice, give thanks, and sing.

We give thanks for the rhythms of music, that make us
want to dance, march, to clap our hands in joy:

Rejoice! Rejoice! Rejoice, give thanks, and sing.

We give thanks for sweet melodies that make us sing
in happiness,
Or that quiet our minds and our spirits,
Or that make lullabies for sleepy babies:

Rejoice! Rejoice! Rejoice, give thanks, and sing.

Most of all do we give thanks for the music that brings
us together,
When we listen
Or when we sing.

Rejoice! Rejoice! Rejoice, give thanks, and sing.

Songs

FOR THE BEGINNING OF THE SERVICE OF WORSHIP

QUIET OUR MINDS*

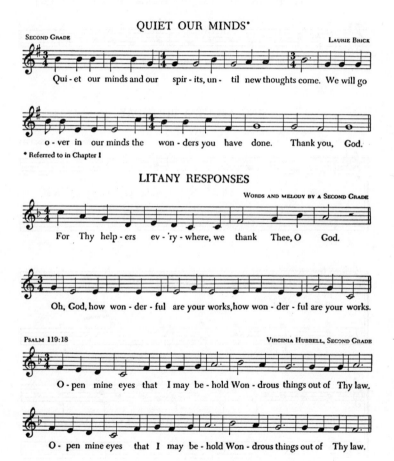

Second Grade

Laurie Brick

Qui - et our minds and our spir - its, un - til new thoughts come. We will go

o - ver in our minds the won - ders you have done. Thank you, God.

* Referred to in Chapter I

LITANY RESPONSES

Words and melody by a Second Grade

For Thy help - ers ev - 'ry - where, we thank Thee, O God.

Oh, God, how won - der - ful are your works, how won - der - ful are your works.

Psalm 119:18

Virginia Hubbell, Second Grade

O - pen mine eyes that I may be - hold Won - drous things out of Thy law.

O - pen mine eyes that I may be - hold Won - drous things out of Thy law.

GOLDEN RULE — FELIX MENDELSSOHN

As ye would that men should do to you, Do ye ev - en so _ un - to them. _

ARMILDA B. KAISER — A. B. K.

Teach us Thy way, O Lord, Teach us Thy way, O Lord,

In all we do, In all we say, Teach us Thy way, O Lord,

SING ABOUT A BIRTHDAY

NANCY BYRD TURNER — ROBERTA BITGOOD, 1944

Sing a - bout a birth - day, Birth - day bright and dear,

Ev - ery bod - y has one, Ev - ery sing - le year.

Birth - days are a time for know - ing Just how much we have been grow - ing,

232

Tall-er, strong-er, kind-er, More gent-le than be-fore,

Sing a-bout a birth-day, Such a hap-py day!

HEALING STRENGTH AND JOY

ALICE M. PULLEN

TRADITIONAL NURSERY RHYME MELODY

1. We praise Thee for the sun, The gold-en shin-ing sun,
2. We praise Thee for the wind, The strong re-fresh-ing wind,

That gives us heal-ing, strength and joy, We praise Thee for the sun.
That gives us heal-ing, strength and joy, We praise Thee for the wind.

We praise Thee for the rain, The soft-ly fall-ing rain,
We praise Thee for Thy love, Our Friend and Fath-er God,

That gives us heal-ing, strength and joy, We praise Thee for the rain.
Who gives us heal-ing, strength and joy, We praise Thee for Thy love.

233

GLAD LET US BE FOR PEOPLE

DORIS GILL

A SECOND GRADE

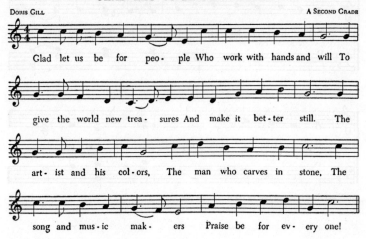

Glad let us be for peo - ple Who work with hands and will To

give the world new trea - sures And make it bet - ter still. The

art - ist and his col - ors, The man who carves in stone, The

song and mus - ic mak - ers Praise be for ev - ery one!

2. Glad let us be for people who find a cure for pain
   And give to folk who need them, new strength and health again;
   The clever man, the doctor, who drives away disease,
   The nurse with healing fingers: glad let us be for these.

3. Praise be for all the brave ones at work for God today
   In forest, farm and city, in mission far away:
   Praise all who with the Father are building well and true
   A world of joy and friendship; come, let us build it, too.

LIFE OUT OF DEATH

WORDS AND MUSIC BY ALICE.M. PULLEN

1. Praise be to God! There comes out of the
2. Praise be to God! There comes out of the
3. Praise be to God! There comes out of the
4. Praise to our Fa - ther God, Giv - er of

night the day, Out of the gloom of
chrys - a - lis dry, Yel - low or blue or
bur - ied grain Won - der - ful life, a
life to all, Won - der - ful life, that

win - ter - time Spring with its flow - ers gay.
snow - y winged, Gay lit - tle but - ter - fly.
hun - dred - fold Har - vest of joy a - gain.
can - not die, Giv - en to great and small!

MAKER OF THE PLANETS

Doris Gill

Alice M. Pullén

1. Mak - er of the plan - ets, hear our song to Thee:
2. Rul - er of all na - tions, hear our song of peace:
3. Fath - er of all peo - ple, hear our song of love:
4. Lord of all cre - a - tion hear our song of joy:

May this world of won - der fol - low Thy de - cree.
May good feel - ing pros - per, Kind - li - ness in - crease.
May the power of friend - ship strong and might - y prove.
May Thy glad - d'ning spir - it dis - con - tent de - stroy.

Sun and moon and star - worlds cease - less - ly o - bey;
Strength - en us in build - ing bridg - es of good - will;
All be - long to Thee, the dus - ky and the fair;
In - to peo - ple's hearts when may be fear or pain,

May we heed Thee faith - ful - ly as they.
Men shall yet Thy laws of peace ful - fill.
Teach us all things e - qual - ly to share.
King of Glo - ry en - ter and re - main.

236

THEY KNEW THE GREEN WOULD COME AGAIN

NANCY BYRD TURNER

A THIRD GRADE

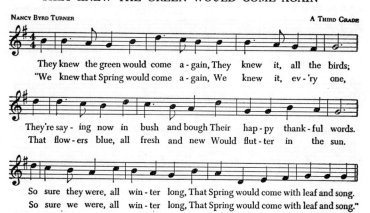

They knew the green would come a - gain, They knew it, all the birds;
"We knew that Spring would come a - gain, We knew it, ev - 'ry one,

They're say - ing now in bush and bough Their hap - py thank - ful words.
That flow - ers blue, all fresh and new Would flut - ter in the sun.

So sure they were, all win - ter long, That Spring would come with leaf and song.
So sure we were, all win - ter long, That Spring would come with leaf and song."

IT COMES EVERY YEAR

NANCY BYRD TURNER

A SECOND GRADE

Who has an - y doubt that Spring's com - ing a - gain?"

"Not I," said the rob - in, "Not I," said the wren.

"Not I," said the child - ren; They had - n't yet seen

an - y buds on the bough, An - y leaves, an - y green,

"But 'twill come," they all said, "Nev - er fear, nev - er fear,

God calls the Spring - time, And it comes ev - 'ry year."

237

SNOW SONG

J. P. B. AND J. S. H. PRIMARY CHILDREN

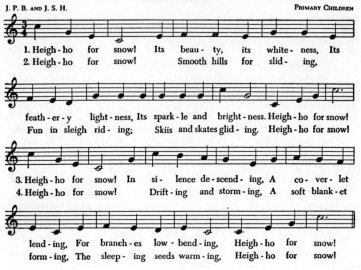

1. Heigh-ho for snow! Its beau-ty, its white-ness, Its
2. Heigh-ho for snow! Smooth hills for slid-ing,

feath-er-y light-ness, Its spark-le and bright-ness. Heigh-ho for snow!
Fun in sleigh rid-ing; Skiis and skates glid-ing. Heigh-ho for snow!

3. Heigh-ho for snow! In si-lence de-scend-ing, A co-ver-let
4. Heigh-ho for snow! Drift-ing and storm-ing, A soft blank-et

lend-ing, For branch-es low-bend-ing, Heigh-ho for snow!
form-ing, The sleep-ing seeds warm-ing, Heigh-ho for snow!

WINTER CREEPS, NATURE SLEEPS

SUO-CAN   WELSH

Win-ter creeps; Na-ture sleeps; Birds are gone, Flowers are none,
God's a-live! Grow and thrive, Hid-den a-way, bloom of May,

Fields are bare, Bleak the air, Leaves are shed; All seems dead.
Robe of June! Ve-ry soon Naught but green Will be seen!

Second Stanza to be sung more quickly

238

JOY IS ABROAD

Words and Music by
Alice M. Pullen

1. Joy is a - broad. Win - ter is o - ver; 'tis Spring of the year.
2. Joy is a - broad Speck - led - breast thrush - es sing sweet - ly and shrill;
3. Joy is a - broad. Gar - dens are wak - ing, and daf - fo - dils gold,
4. Eas - ter is here, Tell - ing us Je - sus is liv - ing and strong,
5. Giv - er of joy, Help us that we may be build - ers of Spring,

Fat buds are burst - ing and green leaves ap - pear. Joy is a - broad!
Brown wren and black - bird with bright yel - low bill. Joy is a - broad.
Trum - pet the tid - ings that death can - not hold. Joy is a - broad!
Show - ing man - kind how to con - quer all wrong. Joy is a - broad!
True peace and glad - ness and ev - 'ry good thing; Till all men sing

Praise to the King, the Cre - a - tor, the life - giv - ing Lord.
Praise to the King, the Cre - a - tor, the life - giv - ing Lord.
Praise to the King, the Cre - a - tor, the life - giv - ing Lord.
Praise to the King, the Cre - a - tor, the life - giv - ing Lord.
Praise to our Fa - ther, Cre - a - tor and life - giv - ing King.

239

ROUND AND ROUND

J. P. BROWN

ARR. FROM ANTONIN DVOŘÁK, 1841-1904

Round and round, Round and round Fol - low night and day,
Round and round, Round and round, Sea - sons come and go,

Sun and shower, Seed and flower In their rhythm - ic way.
Flower of June, Aut - umn moon, Win - ter winds that blow.

Day and night, Dark and light, Rain and sun and rain;
Winds that blow, Melt - ing snow, Op' - ning buds of Spring,

Plants that grow seeds to sow, Plants to bloom a - gain;
Gent - le breeze, Green - ing trees, Nest - ing birds that sing;

Round and round, Round and round, Nev - er - end - ing play:
Sun is high In the sky, Sum - mer days are long;

Once be - gun, Nev - er done, this is Na - ture's way; This is Na - ture's Way.
Now a - gain Au - tumn rain: Nev - er - end - ing song: Nev - er - end - ing song!

240

Index of Titles of Poems, Songs and Prayers

241

Index of First Lines of Poems

244

Index of First Lines of Prayers and Meditations

Index of First Lines of Litanies

O God, how wonderful are your works (A Wonder Litany)—208
O God, we thank thee for light—47
O God whose laws will never change (A Litany to follow talk on law)—75
Oh give thanks unto the Lord (Ps. 136)—46, 174

We thank thee, God, for great humanitarians (Litany incorporating second-grade definitions of great humanitarians)—179
We thank you God for the signs of spring all around us (A Spring Litany of Rejoicing)—202

Index of First Lines of Songs

Index of Stories Outlined or Given in Full

lined), JEANETTE PERKINS BROWN, 126

"He Wants Me to Do It," JEANETTE PERKINS BROWN, 150

How the Four Fishermen Learned (in two parts), JEANETTE PERKINS BROWN, 133, 136

How Harold Helped (outlined in full), ANNIE SILLS BROOKS, 81

How Timothy Found His Place (complete), JEANETTE PERKINS BROWN, 100

Incident from Alice Freeman Palmer's Life, 119

Little Girl with a Light, The, JEANETTE PERKINS BROWN, 49

Little Trot (briefly outlined), A. LICHTENBERGER, 77

One Good Thing, JAMES ENDICOTT, 84

Praying Hands, The (retold), JEANETTE PERKINS BROWN, 89

Purse of Gold and the Seeing Eye, The (outlined), PATTEN BEARD, 118

When Jesus Broke a Circle (incident), JEANETTE PERKINS BROWN, 127

You Pray for What You Can't Buy (incident), ALDEN S. MOSHAMMER, 81

Index of Services of Worship Given in Full or in Part

Index of Authors and Composers

Set in Linotype Caledonia
Format by Edwin H. Kaplin
Manufactured by The Haddon Craftsmen, Inc.
Published by HARPER & BROTHERS, *New York*